STILL
LIFE
IN
CRETE

a singular view

About the Author

Journalist, teacher, cartoonist and maker of idiosyncratic box-art constructions – Anthony Cox has been all these. He started his career in journalism as a London newspaper messenger boy, and ended it, following redundancy from the editorial staff of *The Sunday Times*, as a freelance contributor to various UK publications. As a mature student, he studied for a degree in English and then for a diploma in fine art. His teaching experience embraced work in schools, adult education and universities. The author's academic career came to an end when he took early retirement from the London college where he ran postgraduate courses in print journalism. He happily quit journalism, teaching and England to start his "third age" in the more hospitable climate of western Crete, where he now lives in a mountain village with his wife and their two pug dogs.

STILL LIFE IN

CRETE

a singular view
- with illustrations by the author -
Anthony Cox

VNIVERSAL PVBLISHERS

First published in the USA in 2001
by Universal Publishers

ISBN 1-58112-691-3

Universal Publishers/ uPUBLISH.com
Florida USA 2001

www.upublish.com/books/cox-a.htm

For Clare, my daughter

CHAPTER ONE

The property market was depressed and so were we.

Waiting for us in Crete was an old stone-and-rubble shack, last inhabited by a mule called Turnip. This was where we wanted to be, where we planned to build a house and a new life. Turnip had enjoyed what we now wanted for ourselves. At the boundary of our Cretan property, a dry-stone wall enclosed an olive grove where the trees flashed silver-tipped leaves in the mountain breeze. Beyond, the land fell away to the infinitely blue Mediterranean. Where there was no dazzling sea, there was a scattered patchwork of more dry-stone walls, olive groves and vineyards, randomly punctuated by the natural exclamation marks of stately cypress trees. Meandering sheep grazed the craggy lower slopes of the mountains that all but surrounded us. From the sun-bathed shack we could revel in the sweet aroma of our own fig trees and enjoy the melodious tinkling of distant goat-bells. Sound travelled sharp and clear through the limpid air, but the shack was at the end of an agricultural track; the only car we would hear would be our own and, although we were part of a mountain village, our neighbours were mostly out of sight.

Standing in the way of all this was a 200-year-old thatched cottage in Kent. The local conservation officer had described it as "a fine example of a yeoman farmhouse" and our friends claimed that they envied us our ownership. The oddly named Gypsy Court was a pretty little place of character – most of it genuine. It was a chocolate-box house, admittedly more of the Cadbury's Roses variety than some more upmarket confection, but its major drawback was its location: it was in the cabbage-rich flatlands of east Kent, where roses did not flourish and the outlook was more often drizzling than dazzling. For months on end we were surrounded by pungent yeoman crops of sprouts. Our six acres of tree-less land provided no barrier to the evil, miasmic stench of slowly-rotting brassica, while the mist-laden view across the bare plains of England's eastern front did nothing to lift our spirits during the seemingly-endless bleak and damp winter months. The thought of years of mortgage payments gave us palpitations and the widespread Kentish enthusiasm for scattering agrochemicals threatened worse. It was a catalogue of gloom and it offered no challenge to Crete's promise of aromatic fig trees and the peerless sight of the pink-tinted peaks of the White Mountains every long summer evening. We were waiting to escape.

Between the mule's stone-and-rubble shack and our thatched cottage there was a story to tell. It began with a simple plan: to live an uncomplicated life in the sun and to make a slender income stretch to the end of each month unaided by overdrafts or the playing of credit cards. The problem of money had already been solved, thanks to an unexpected opportunity to "down-size". Following a dispute of mind-boggling inconsequentiality, I had been offered early retirement from a job as a college lecturer. The pension on offer was almost as piddling as the matter that had led to it being offered, but, if we were careful, I knew that we could use it to change our lives. Susan would be able to wave goodbye to grindingly-long hours at the computer end of the market research business and I could return to an early enthusiasm: art. It was an opportunity that might never come again. I put up my hand for the pension. I was only 46 and sound enough in wind and limb. We calculated that we could stay afloat – but only in the Mediterranean. And only after selling the cottage in Kent...

The second problem – where to go? – had also been easily solved. We had narrowed our search down to an area no bigger than 130,800 square kilometres! Tuscany and Provence might beckon others but we preferred the earthier and more affordable promise of Greece. First, we had done our sums and knew that it was definitely a country where our money would stretch. My weekly pension translated into about twice what an illegal Balkan immigrant would earn for six days work. I just had to hope that the drachma and the £ never reached parity otherwise we'd be sweating alongside the gangs of itinerant foreign labourers who scraped a living from olive picking and shovelling who-knows-what. Secondly, we liked the Greeks, who seemed devoid of the forced niceties of so much English behaviour and were warm, spontaneous, open and expressive – and often robustly so. Perhaps the more hospitable climate had something to do with it! We also liked Greek wine and the ready availability of cheap, locally produced foodstuffs, which came and went with the seasons. The survival of traditional peasant-farms meant that a lot of one's food could be seen growing in numerous small fields – or "on the hoof". But there was another reason for Greece's siren call. An earlier marriage had endowed Susan with Greek citizenship and, eventually, knowledge of the language. The first was of little consequence; now that we all live together in Euroland we are more-or-less free to come and go as we please. The ability to speak the language was more useful. I already spoke "evening-class advanced beginners" Greek and so together we were able to make others understand our wants, dislikes and aversions. Without the language we could still have managed, albeit more slowly but that wouldn't have been a problem in Greece, where – at least outside Athens – "slowly, slowly" is as common an expression as London's "Get a move on, will you!"

Greece may be smaller than, say, Alabama, but it's still a big place for home-hunters. Turnip's old shack was not easily found and before we stumbled upon it, we took many wrong turnings – although we always knew that we were on the right road in planning to move to Greece! Our best-laid plan was to move from A to B in a straight and unobstructed line which involved selling Gypsy Court quickly and – just as quickly – realising our dream in Greece. It didn't work like that, but then best-laid plans seldom do.

Trying to sell an under-sized house in east Kent's stagnant housing market proved to be the one problem for which Greek-style patience was the only answer. Our first attempt to appoint an estate agent was inauspicious. It began and ended with one of those irritating telephone conversations where the person you want to speak to won't speak directly to you. I spoke to his secretary, she spoke to him, he spoke to her, she spoke to me.

"What's the address of the property?" she asked. I tried to explain: "It hasn't really got an address. It's in a country lane with no name. The cottage is called Gypsy Court." She shouted across at her boss: "It's a gypsy cart!" I heard his answer before she relayed it to me: "Tell him we don't deal with mobile homes." The next agent didn't use a go-between and we got on much better. While the months slipped by and the photograph of the cottage slowly faded in his window display, we used the time for house-hunting expeditions to Greece. We concentrated on the large island of Evia, which Susan had known and liked, and parts of the mainland within reach of Athens. We avoided the smaller islands because we had heard of the rigours of island life in the wet winter months, with nearly everything shut down, most of the population gone and public services just ticking over, at best. Nothing really appealed, just bits here and there, but the downsides of life in Greece were ever-present and they put a damper on my enthusiasm. I once saw a newspaper headline proclaiming: "GREEKS ARE FAT – IT'S OFFICIAL". Another fundamental truth – GREEKS ARE NOISY! – hasn't yet made it on to the front pages. I remember the start of a new evening class season in London. The Greek language tutor had opened the classroom window to admit some air, but instead the mighty roar of the rush-hour traffic poured in. He carried on regardless, but then he would – he was a Greek! One of the students wanted the window closed. "Why?" asked the tutor. "Because it's noisy," answered the innocent student. The tutor laughed and said, "You're going to Greece – you'd better get used to noise!" Greece is not quiet; neither is it a land of temples and flowers. Ancient Greece is now ancient history. The countryside is filthy with the half-finished skeletons of modern block-houses surrounded by the detritus of their building. Concrete not marble is the distinctive construction material of modern Greece, that plus rusty iron reinforcing rods, which seem to jut out of every bit of cement ever poured. We liked Greece but that didn't mean that we could accept every anti-social excess, every abuse of the environment, every ugly building. We wanted to be happy with our surroundings and we felt sure that somewhere in Greece we would find what we wanted. We would definitely know our new home when we saw it, but we hadn't seen it yet. Perhaps we were looking in the wrong places...

The newspapers claimed that UK property sales were on the up, but it seemed that east Kent had opted out of their surveys. We had obviously deluded ourselves that the estate agent's "in-particulars" – the ancient well, the inglenook, the old brick-built bread oven, oak beams and the refurbished cream-and-black 1954 Aga – would guarantee a rapid sale of Gypsy Court. When we bought the house these delights were hidden or falling down. Our successful excavation of them had led us to think, in our excitement, that we'd discovered a gold mine, but the first of our eventual handful of viewers didn't start a gold rush. The original parchment deed of 1794 was no substitute for a decent-sized second bedroom. The truth was becoming painfully obvious: the house was too small, impossible to extend in any worthwhile way, in the wrong place *and* our asking price was too high. The agent, however, was an optimist who saw no point in dropping the price because the house would still be too small, impossible to extend and definitely in the wrong place. Like Mr Micawber, he fully expected somebody to turn up, eventually. We came very near to abandoning our plan to move to Greece, but decided to make just one more trip abroad. We left the house keys with the agent – and our two pug dogs in the local kennels. There was no doubt that these trips were eating into our funds; this would have to be the last one. If we couldn't find our place in the sun this time, we would give up and try Plan B: move to a cheaper house in Cornwall (heads) or Scotland (tails), invest in good quality waterproofs and thick underwear – and accept the inevitability of expensive heating bills. Of course, we would still have to sell the "gypsy cart", but we believed, along with our agent, that we would – eventually! We desperately wanted to find somewhere. Crete was a part of Greece unknown to either of us. Susan's former married name had been Angelaki, which was of Cretan origin and meant "little angel". As we set off, we reminded ourselves of this and hoped that it was an omen that someone up there would be looking out for us.

Our initial destination was Hania, the administrative centre of western Crete. A fine old seaport city, occupied in turn by Venetians, Turks and Germans – with many of the latter apparently still there! We booked into a hotel converted from a Venetian house. The room was large and airy, the bed comfortable and the view, northwards across the harbour to the lighthouse and out over the Cretan Sea, was spectacular. Intuitively, we felt that we might be getting close to what we wanted. Our decision to take an evening walk along the wide promenade around the harbour gave that warm feeling a jolt. We seemed to be the only people not mindlessly circling about on spluttering motorbikes, mopeds or scooters. We sought escape in the narrow back streets, which were thronged with tourists. The prospect of dinner, our first meal in Crete, led us away from the bustling old harbour area and its strings of tavernas, each with an unappealing tout accosting passers-by. We overhead one huckster inviting a couple to check out "the quality of the people we have eating here"! We had no recommendations, but close to the ruin of the Venetian arsenal we found a tout-less taverna that was busy enough with local Haniotes to look as if it might be a good place to eat real food. It was. We settled on *saganaki* (fried cheese) and *syglina* (smoked pork), *paidakia* (lamb chops) and *horiatiki salata* (seasonal mixed salad). Because the weather was hot, the taverna served a crisp, fresh rosé house wine rather than the more usual robust straight-from-the-barrel red. It was an excellent accompaniment to a simple meal prepared with a lightness of touch unusual in Greek cuisine. When we asked for the bill, the waiter brought us a decanter of a pleasantly smooth *raki*, better-known in Crete as *tschikoudia*, and a plate of small, fluffy baklava, neither of which appeared on the bill. Although the place was filling up, no one showed any hurry to take our money. After another leisurely *tschikoudia* each we made our way out into the warm summer night to stroll around the warren of tiny streets before returning to the hotel. We sat for a while on our balcony before turning in. It was only half-past-ten but we were tired. Very tired, but very satisfied.

The blast hit us at midnight. Hammer blows whacked rhythmically around our heads. The bed vibrated. Boots stomped.

We were trapped in the aural hell of a hotel room above a disco! We tried the power of positive thinking, we tried stuffing our pillows in our ears, but nothing would make the noise abate. I went to get the hotel manager. He knew what I wanted before I even said it. Half-an-hour later we were back in bed in another room on an upper floor. Bliss! No disco!

Three hours later I was woken by the sound of someone falling on the wooden stairs just outside our room. Loud female giggling and a baritone guffawing suggested that it wasn't serious. The room next door was obviously theirs. I groaned as they splashed around in their bathroom. This was going to be a night to forget. I looked across at Susan. Fast asleep! I could hear every sound from next door. Their bed creaked and its headboard tapped and then banged against the wall. He grunted, she moaned – and after the wall had been pierced by a shrill, climactic "yes...yeS...yES...YES...Y-E-E-S-S-S!" I sighed alongside them in post-coital relief. I stared at the ceiling and thought of sleep, but not for long. They were at it again! Who were these people? This time they had moved across their room to try out another piece of creaking furniture. He seemed to be pacing himself with a metronome: creak...creak...creak... I looked at my watch. Five o'clock. What a performer! At six, I could stand it no longer. I went to the window and threw open the shutters. The creaking was louder. Cautiously, I looked out. Next-door's shutters were only half-closed and in the crisp, early-morning light I could see what was happening. The breeze from the sea was gently moving one shutter on a rusty hinge: creak...creak...creak... I had been wrong; it was definitely a night to remember.

I waited until seven and woke Susan, who was blissfully unaware of the night's adventures. I decided that I had lost interest in Hania – we'd never want to live in a city anyway – and she agreed that we should make an early start on our planned drive eastwards, towards Rethimnon. But that would be after we had been out for breakfast. We searched in vain for the same sustaining traditional breakfast we had eaten at *kafenea* on the mainland: Greek coffee and a glass of milk, a lump of coarse, village bread and a plate of honey, in which sat a knob of white butter, distinguished by its slightly rancid taste. In Hania, we could find only the ubiquitous Euro-breakfast of cold, factory-made "toast", fruit juice, coffee, cake, caterer's-pack butter-pats and little plastic tubs of apricot jam and honey, with razor-thin slices of processed cheese and meat.

The drive to Rethimnon took us through the area known as Apokorona, much favoured by foreigners moving to Crete and therefore unlikely to satisfy us, particularly our need to live as cheaply as possible. The arrival of foreigners in any numbers puts up prices everywhere in Greece so whatever the reputed appeal of Apokorona, we decided to give it a miss. The coastal route along the northern shore of Crete had its moments but we were glad to arrive in Rethimnon, where we planned to stay the night. We relaxed for a while in the peaceful, verdant public gardens and then wandered the bustling streets of the old city. Rethimnon's charm was palpable, but despite the city's medieval character I noted at least three discos.

We had a recommendation for an allegedly quiet hotel but search as we might, we could not find it. A moustachioed Rethimniot leaning in the doorway of a small *kafeneon* observed us quizzically. Susan responded to his raised eyebrow and asked if he knew of the hotel. "Come with me," he said and led us around the corner into a small courtyard. The hotel was there but its door was firmly shut. "Stavro!" yelled our Rethimniot. No answer. "STAVRO!" Louder, but still no reply. We came to discover that this was the Cretan way of calling on someone, even if their door had both knocker and bell. "He will return soon. Let me give you a drink while you wait." Back in the *kafeneon*, our new friend disappeared behind the bar and reappeared with a bottle of *tschikoudia*, three small glasses and a handful of peanuts with salt on their shells. We were about to say no to his offer of a fourth dram when he was startled out of his chair by the arrival of a black-clad barrel of a woman who glared at the *tschikoudia* bottle and then at us. Our Rethimniot abandoned us. The woman's ferocious glare seemed to require an answer. "We're waiting…we were just having a drink with the *kafeneon* owner," I explained. "He is the barber from next door! I…I am the owner!" she shouted, indignantly stabbing her ample chest with the fingers of one hand while scissoring the air with the fingers of the other. I offered to pay for the drinks. After a little more huffing-and-puffing she calmed down: "He's always doing that. Don't worry – I'll make him pay!" She tried to press another *tschikoudia* on us but because we were both up to our limit of raw liquor on an empty stomach we made our excuses and left.

Stavros had come back from wherever he had been and we took one of his rooms for the night. After an unremarkable lunch, save for the fact that the proprietor snootily declared that his taverna didn't serve olives, we made a further exploration of old Rethimnon. One of the rarest sights in Greece is a public lavatory when you want one. However, across the road the municipal art gallery looked like the answer. It cost us 500 drachmas each to get in but I consoled myself with thoughts of a clean WC and a look at the art of Rethimnon. I was to be disappointed on two counts. It was an exhibition of exactly the same sort of stuff one could see in "contemporary" galleries all over Europe. Maybe we had had too much to drink and our perceptions were dulled but neither of us could work up any enthusiasm for what was happening: on display were six separate TV screens each showing the same moody-looking fellow slowly blowing up balloons. Why six? It was a typical example of run-of-the-loop "video art", the now far-from-high-tech equivalent of watching paint dry. There were also some paintings that looked as if they had been retched up; one of them was actually called, *"Untitled (sic)"*! The biggest disappointment of all was that the gallery had no lavatory.

The hotel was quiet but breakfast was the same as in Hania. Today we had a detour planned; we were heading for Perama and a small village just beyond it famed for its cave. A Cretan acquaintance of ours had returned to the village from many years in America and to demonstrate the enterprising spirit he had imbibed there had offered to be the guardian of Melidoni's cave in return for the concession of selling food and drink to its visitors. As we drove into Perama we passed an agricultural truck driving in the opposite direction. We looked at each other as if to say, "Did you see that?" The driver was 12 if he was a day! Perama, we later learned, is at the centre of a region notorious for its reputedly scant regard of the law. If that was true, we somehow managed to pass through unscathed. No one held us up at pistol point or offered to sell us a lorry-load of cannabis, but the place did have a tangible "High Noon" air. We found Marcus, our acquaintance, at home, snoozing in his courtyard under a tree, which was growing both oranges and lemons. We had planned a flying visit but he insisted that we saw the cave, the village and stayed for the night.

It was late morning and his wife and daughters were already busy serving tourists at the family *kantina* outside the cave, which was like lots of Greek caves: deep, dank and dark. Back outside in the blistering sunlight we asked Marcus what the attraction was. He said, "This, my friends, is where Talos, the ancient bull-headed guardian of Crete, lived!" Of course it was. We sat and drank coffee, watching the tourists arrive. Marcus had been given leaflets on the cave's history, printed in English, Greek and German and he handed these out, trying to match the language to the visitor. A young German couple – easily identified – went off into the cave, clutching their leaflet… Some 20 minutes later they returned and solemnly approached Marcus. "We want to apologise," said the young man. "Ah, yes," said Marcus. "Terrible, terrible things were done by the nazis during the war," said the young man. Marcus stretched himself and in a relaxed don't-worry-about-it voice replied: "War is war, my young friend." The young man, with his girlfriend nervously holding his hand, nodded a somewhat confused agreement. After they had driven away, Marcus explained that this often happened. Although it was the Turks of old who had massacred hundreds of innocent people in the cave, the apologetic young German – along with a lot of his compatriots before him – had misread the leaflet and assumed that the nazis were to blame. Perhaps a guilt complex is part of the modern German psyche.

Later, we walked around the village with Marcus. I asked him why there were so many *kafenea* for such a small population. He pointed out a sombre, brown-ish place. "That's the right-wing *kafeneon*," he said. The next one looked like a youth club. A noisy one with men and women smoking and arguing – and doing both equally furiously – turned out to be the allegedly left-wing *kafeneon*. Away from them all was a cosy-looking place with two elderly men dozing at separate tables. "And that one?" I asked. "Ah, that's the neutral *kafeneon*," Marcus chuckled, obviously enjoying his own joke. I asked him which one he patronised. "In a Cretan village you're obliged to visit them all," he said, diplomatically.

Over an excellent dinner of boiled rice and chicken – the traditional Cretan *pilafi* – cooked by Marcus, we discussed our plans. Our hosts were convinced that their village was the only place to live in the whole of Crete and they knew of a "sweet little house" that was empty and cheap and waiting for a tenant. The village was interesting enough at first glance – and friendly – but its position, hemmed in by scrubby hills on which a constant summertime fire watch had to be maintained, made it very hot and air-less – and it was nowhere near the sea. It wasn't what we wanted. Nevertheless, out of politeness, we agreed to look at the vacant house.

The next morning, Marcus reported that no one quite knew the whereabouts of the key but that it would be found and would arrive sometime during the day. We didn't want to hang around Melidoni and so we persuaded him to show us the outside of the house. It was built from breeze-blocks – hot in summer, cold and damp in winter – and was redeemed only by a small courtyard with a lemon tree. It definitely wasn't what we wanted! Marcus agreed that it wasn't really a very attractive house... However, he offered to take us on a short excursion to a "fascinating" place he was certain would appeal to us.

We arrived in an area of olive groves from the midst of which rose a small hill topped by a group of old houses. A winding footpath took us through the trees, up the hill and into what had been an isolated hamlet. Clustered together were about 15 traditional houses built from dressed stone and with massive olivewood beams. All were in various stages of disrepair with overgrown gardens and walls ruptured by burgeoning fig trees. None of the remaining doors, which were all studded with antique ironwork, were locked. We wandered from house to house, each one a gem awaiting restoration. All the rooms were filthy and many still contained bits of dilapidated and wormy furniture. From under a collapsed iron bedstead I pulled out a battered and ancient suitcase. It was empty but for a few faded photographs, the best one of which I salvaged. It was a grimy, postcard-sized studio portrait of a soldier. It had been taken in 1940 at Komotini, on Greece's northern frontier. The soldier was framed by a heart that sported a sad little verse:

> *The letter I sent you is lost*
> *and also forgotten*
> *So I send you my little body*
> *which is unforgettable*

Perhaps it was more optimistic than sad! Any further poking around was interrupted by the arrival of a man who politely asked us not to take any of the furniture. We readily agreed. Our visitor claimed that the hamlet had been abandoned after a feud had broken out between the inhabitants. His account of events made a good story, touching as it did on the notorious Cretan tradition of the vendetta. He said that he was related to one of the families that had left and now he kept half-an-eye on the decaying houses. We left wishing we could find such a place – in the right location – for ourselves. We thanked Marcus for an interesting excursion. "My pleasure," he said.

That night we were in Iraklion, the noisy, traffic-clogged capital of Crete and Greece's fourth largest city. It was uncomfortably hot so we booked into a big hotel that offered air conditioning. The city has lots of fast-food joints, all by definition to be avoided but particularly the one whose English sign boasted, possibly with unconscious honesty, "HUGE VARIETY IN QUALITY!" We had our dinner at a *psistaria* – a charcoal grill, where the service is not much slower than in a fast-food outlet but where the dishes are infinitely tastier. The seats are more comfortable, too, which was important to us because we wanted to sit and review our plan, which had been to drive eastwards along the northern coast, stopping short of Agios Nikolaos, and the notorious, tourist-infested waters of the "Cretan Riviera". The time spent with Marcus had not been wasted; it had helped us to focus better on what we were looking for. We wanted to be within sight of the sea and within easy reach of a good-sized town; we definitely didn't want to lose our identity in a place where for half of the year hordes of tourists blinded shops and tavernas to everything except making a fast drachma. Neither of us felt very positive about what we were seeing. The further east we travelled from Hania the bigger and busier everything seemed to get – from the roads to the hotels and the blocks of holiday apartments. I flicked through our guidebook for inspiration. I had often thought that guidebooks in general should carry a warning: "Reading this book may lead to a disappointing anti-climax should you follow its recommendations." That was why we had not taken as gospel a remark in our book, which I now read out for us to reconsider. It claimed that two "great chunks" were still "blissfully free of the crowds and commercialism": western Crete and the villages of central Crete. I checked the date of publication: 1994. Could it still be true? We resolved to head back to Hania to find out; in any case, we felt that we would be wasting our time looking eastwards. Now that we had a clear destination in view, we decided to finish off the evening with a visit to an unusual find: a pastry shop serving an Athenian delicacy, *loucoumades* (honey puffs). Served with a glass of water and made while you wait, they're deliciously light and fluffy, dusted with cinnamon and dripping with honey. Such self-indulgence left us feeling we really shouldn't leave Iraklion without dutifully visiting the city's most famous find, the ancient Minoan palace of Knossos, and, because we'd had a second helping of *loucoumades* between us, we resolved to take in the archaeological museum as well.

⟨HAPTER TWO

Hania was in sight but the nail in the piece of wood in the middle of the road wasn't. Fortunately our hire-car came to a halt right outside a tyre fitter's workshop and I was spared the horror of a roadside wheel-change in the heat and dust, fending-off glancing blows from speeding lorries. The puncture repair was quick and cheap and the fitter gave me his card "for the next time". I looked at it; it was in English. I read out in loud disbelief: "'Discount 15% in springily with weighted free'?" "That's right," he beamed. I don't suppose I would have done any better in Greek – but then I wouldn't have tried, not in print, anyway!

We had already decided to find a place to stay in Hania and to make daily sorties in search of somewhere to live. We parked outside the building of the *Pankritikos Omilos Vrakophoron* – The All-Cretan Association of Baggy Pant-Wearers! Susan wondered what they got up to inside. "Which? Their pants or the building?" I asked. "It doesn't matter. Quick!" she hissed. "It's that woman from the flight out." I recognised the woman in time to follow Susan's quick sidestep into a doorway. Our charter plane's in-flight menu had promised roast chicken but the captain broadcast a last-minute substitution: cottage pie. Orders to bale out would have been greeted with more enthusiasm. The woman in the aisle seat next to Susan lunged at a passing stewardess, who patiently explained that because of a mix-up in the catering department the plane had been loaded with a cargo of cottage pie. "I don't care about that," said the woman. "I don't want cottage pie." "Are you a vegetarian, madam?" asked the stewardess. "No, I'm a passenger and I don't want cottage pie," she insisted. I had thought about suggesting that if she closed her eyes while eating she wouldn't be able to tell the difference, but the stewardess was still in control: "I'll see what I can do," she smiled sweetly. The woman turned to Susan and confided that she'd been on a self-assertiveness course and was "kicking arse and liking it". Susan was just about to exert herself and make a riposte when the stewardess returned with a cheese salad, apparently conjured out of the ether. The triumphant smirk on the woman's face widened as the rest of us pulled back the tinfoil coverings of our soggy mash-and-mince and a smell of school-dinner rolled through the plane. Thankfully, her path did not cross our doorway hideout.

This time we decided to stay in rooms. "Rooms" abound in Greece, mostly as simple bed & breakfast-type accommodation – although usually without the breakfast! If you're lucky you can find a bed-sitting room with a kitchenette and a shower, although, sadly, these are now rapidly being replaced by more expensive modern "studios", "suites" and apartments. We returned to the older parts of the city and began knocking at houses bearing the sign "rooms to let". There were plenty of rooms but not with kitchens. If we couldn't have a kitchen, we might as well stay in a hotel. We tried one. It had been painted with coffee flung straight from the cup, the beds were punitive and the corridors were alive to the sound of rampaging Greek teenagers on a poorly-supervised school trip. We went straight back "on the knocker". Within minutes, Irini's eponymous rooms offered us exactly what we wanted, except that not all the rings on the cooker worked – and there were only two! The bedding, apart from the sheets, was in need of refreshment but because the nights were so warm we didn't anticipate using any of it.

For breakfast we had what we wanted: Kerkira butter – the white one with the slightly rancid taste, Cretan thyme honey, a real, crusty loaf that was so hot when purchased that it had to be tossed from hand to hand, and freshly-ground Greek coffee. The shops were open very early so all of this was bought well before 8 am. Irini's cooker offered a big saucepan ring and a tiny one solely for Greek coffee-making. Luckily, it was the small one that worked.

Before setting off on our first exploration of the west, we browsed the classified ads in the main local newspaper, the *Haniotika Nea*. There appeared to be lots of properties for sale – houses old and new, building plots, fields, vineyards and olive groves – but the ads were generally short on details and seldom mentioned price.

Although we had not yet seen anything looking remotely like an English estate agent's office, the newspaper showed that there were such places here. We were impatient to get out so we left the newspaper for later.

We had been wandering around a village on the Akrotiri peninsula, admiring various houses and their luxuriant gardens, when we were offered a property deal! We had been stopped in our tracks by a goat, whose head was sticking out of what looked like a heap of rubble. The goat was amiable and obviously enjoyed a chat with visitors. Then her – maybe his – owner appeared and after exchanging the usual pleasantries unexpectedly asked if we were interested in buying a goat. I told him that we weren't looking for a goat at this time but, impulsively seizing the opportunity of the moment, I said that what we really wanted was a house. "That's okay," he said. "I can keep the goat." He then waved his hand at the heap of rubble and said, "But you're in luck. I'm selling this as a holiday home." We looked at the heap of rubble and then at each other. He obviously wasn't very good at reading body language. "I know what you're thinking. It's not big enough, eh? Well, you're in even more luck. This goat shed – er, little house – is joined to another one. I own that, too. They're what you'd call semi-detached. If you bought them both, they could be knocked together to make you a dream home!" he said with glee. I wanted to ask him if there was another goat next door and whether the two of them were good neighbours, but, "How much?" seemed a more relevant question. "They're 2,000,000 drachmas each, but," he paused, "you can have both for 4,000,000 drachmas." This was our first example of the simplicity of Cretan calculations: one just thinks of a figure and doubles it! We told him we'd sleep on his offer and he replied by telling us what we were to hear again and again: "Don't leave it too long – I've got a German who's interested..." In the new Cretan mythology, every German visitor is a well-heeled punter searching for a second home. English house-hunters soon get tired of the cash-sniffing mantra: "Are you from Germany? No? From Switzerland maybe?" After a few of these interrogative encounters, Susan said she would check on the Greek for, "We are from Ulaanbaatar."

On the drive back to Hania we agreed that so far this part of Planet Earth hadn't actually moved for us. Admittedly, we had seen very little of Crete but we were, as yet, untouched by its reputed magic. The bustling and winding streets of old Hania were, of course, very seductive, but we wouldn't want to live in them. We still had to follow the guidebook and head west, much further west. We discussed estate agents, mostly negatively, nevertheless we thought they might be useful to us here and we resolved to visit a few to see if they could mark our cards. As I parked the car, I saw the sign for a "Real Estate Agent". Was this Fate at work? Although it was late in the evening, most shops and offices were open, including this one. The agent received us at a desk on which sat a blinking mobile 'phone and an overflowing ashtray. On the wall, a calendar – the gift of a cesspit-emptying firm – still showed the previous month. It was the only thing to suggest that the office's business might be linked to property. After trotting quickly through the initial civilities, we said that we were specifically looking for an old house to restore. Although this wasn't strictly true – we would consider anything – we thought it would be a good test of the agent's worth. It was. He showed his hand far too quickly: "What's your spend?" he growled, while fingering a medallion the size of an Olympic gold for line-shooting. Although he was speaking English, it was a variant not immediately obvious to me and I had to ask him what he meant. "How much?" he spat. He was not a pleasant person. Susan knocked 25 per cent off our budgeted figure and he responded with a disparaging sound, rather like a flatulent old bulldog who'd had too much leftover Christmas turkey: "Pfurrrghhh…You won't get anything for that! You couldn't even get a goat shed!" Earlier in the day our money would have bought four goat sheds, even at the inflated prices being asked by the goat-owner. "You'll need more than that if you want to live here! It's very fashionable. Tuscany's nothing now; Crete's the place! Can't you raise any more?" he both mocked and challenged. We looked at each other and then at him; we didn't like or trust him. "No," we said in unison. He started to roll himself a cigarette, narrowing his eyes quizzically at us as he licked the gummed edge of the paper. He obviously thought we were worth spending some time on despite our claimed lack of cash. "For people like you an old house would be good. Plenty of character – but you'll need 50,000,000 drachmas just for the builders," he warned. This sounded like nonsense. Back in Melidoni, Marcus had told us something of Cretan building costs. An unskilled foreign labourer could be had for about 8,000 drachmas a day. With 50,000,000 drachmas we could build ourselves a pyramid! Our agent returned to his spiel: "Of course, if you had the money, you wouldn't have to worry. I'd do everything for you. I'd have to; you'd be like lambs to the slaughter trying to do it on your own. You know, Greeks can be very slippery – and what a language!" Susan interrupted his pitch to tell him – in fluent Greek! – that she spoke fluent Greek. Rigor set in around the half-smile on the agent's thin lips and his eyelids started blinking in time with the light on his mobile 'phone. "Ah, that's good for you..." he hissed. Realising that we would never become pushover clients of his, the blinking switched to a butterfly-fluttering of the eyelids and he looked away, just like a geisha girl pretending demureness. He then terminated our meeting by suddenly jumping to his feet, jiggling his belt, sliding his hand down the front of his trousers and, while scratching himself, breezily announcing, "I'll give you some advice for nothing. Take a look at the Peloponnese – that's cheap! There's not much I can do for you." Hygienic considerations obliged us to dodge his proffered hand. Outside, Susan said, "You know, I think he really wanted to say, 'There's not much I can *do you* for'!" We gave Hania's estate agents the benefit of the doubt and concluded that the medallion man was probably atypical, but we decided against making a trawl of their offices.

After an inexpensive dinner of *kalamarikia* (squid) and *patates* – the Greek equivalent of fish and chips – accompanied by a small, chilled bottle of the local wine co-op's retsina, dry-ish but not at all astringent, we took a stroll through the narrow, teeming, bazaar-like shopping streets of old Hania. On such summer evenings in such places all over Tourist Europe there is a kind of madness abroad. It's not just the sense of everyone around killing the time between dinner and sleep by dawdling from shop to shop on a slow-motion spending spree, it's more what they're invited to spend their "holiday money" on. The buying of souvenirs and gifts is one of tourism's rituals, rather like wearing a zippered-pouch on the belly and looking like a pregnant kangaroo or trying a vile, technicoloured cocktail with a little paper umbrella stuck in it. These activities are harmless enough, and entertaining to the spectator, but what's the point of an Australian *didgeridoo* as a gift from Crete? Amid the banal and the bizarre, there will always be some interesting and unusual indigenous purchases to be made: a spiky, green, white and yellow ceramic cactus, an old iron door lock with a massive key, a piece of Cretan hand-made lace – these at least make some sense as local souvenirs. What, though, are "genuine" Arctic "Eskimo" fur mittens doing in tourist shops in the Mediterranean? Or "authentic art, crafts, paintings and jewellery" from "the Navajo, Hopi and Zuni Indians from America"? Do Native Americans flog their visitors "authentic Cretan baggy pants", crude little "hand-crafted" busts of the Cretan-born statesman Eleftherios Venizelos or cassettes of Nana Mouskouri singing Hadjidakis? Maybe they do, but I doubt it. Perhaps when I live here I'll sell little phials of absolutely nothing labelled "Essential Natural Essence of Tibetan Buddhism" – or some such guff. I bet I'd still have customers if I labelled the phials with the words "ABSOLUTELY NOTHING"! Daft, I call it, but then it's a free market...

Before turning in, Susan carefully scrutinised the newspaper's classified advertisement columns. "It's very strange but apart from some olive groves there doesn't actually seem to be anything for sale in the far west of Crete," she said. This discovery presented us with a dilemma: should we just head westwards to reconnoitre or would we be better off leaving our reconnaissance until after we had found at least one house for sale there? If there weren't any houses to buy and things were still as the guidebook had said, we thought we might feel rather cheated. We were happy enough where we were – at least for a day or two – and so we decided that we would, after all, do the rounds of Hania's estate agents in the morning. If they had nothing to show us, then we would set out to discover for ourselves, whatever the consequences, if the west was still "blissfully free of the crowds and commercialism".

The estate agents we called on were nothing like the one we'd met, either to look at or in their attitude. They had busy offices and an enthusiasm for selling houses rather than ridiculing potential buyers. Unfortunately, most of the properties seemed to be town houses either in or around Hania. We repeated our demands: quietly situated, close to a town, a sea-view and an affordable price but now we added that we wanted it to be well to the west of the island. Nobody rubbished our plan or said it couldn't be done but it seemed that we had picked the most difficult area in which to find a house. The agency we liked best overlooked one of Hania's many challenging traffic junctions. Its first floor office sat like a ship's bridge above the bustling streets and the agent himself was like its captain. He came across as solidly reliable. His beard and moustache were trimmed to perfection, his blazer and tie immaculate and he sported – apparently all the time – a curly pipe from which floated the aroma of scented tobacco. Susan coughed a lot, but I was in sympathy with the agent. I had spent some years of contentment with a couple of silver-mounted curly Petersens, puffing my way through such brands as Troost, Holland House and Amphora, making the house smell like a custard-powder factory. My enthusiasm for such things eventually wafted away but the agent's was obviously undiminished and he had become a connoisseur. Before we could get down to business we had to tell him what England had to offer in the way of sweet-smelling pipe tobaccos. He tried to make a note of my recommendation, the aromatic "Dick Brown's Mixture" from "Dick Brown's, Sandwich"; but whether it was the name of the mixture, the name of the Kentish shop or the fact that he would have to buy it by mail order that made him blink, I couldn't tell. "Never mind," he said, eventually. He then went through the details of what we wanted and told us that he would see what he could do. He asked us to return the next day – or the day after.

We were now back where we started with nothing to do but set out and see what we might find. If we were going west tomorrow, today we'd make an excursion southwards. We had a day of enjoyable motoring on spectacular – and fortunately quiet – mountain roads, with pleasant stops for refreshment in local *kafenea*. We also had an unusual lunch. We stopped in a tiny village where there was but one place to eat and that day the only thing on the menu was fried eggs. We expressed our disappointment and the woman owner said, rather hesitantly, "Well, you can have *fassolada* (bean soup) if you want. I've cooked it for the family and there's enough for two more." We sat down to bowls of this Cretan peasant standby, with bread and glasses of red wine. It was delicious and filling. When we came to pay, our cook said, "Oh, I don't know..." and ended up charging us the equivalent of 50p each! Just out of interest, we asked her if she knew of any houses for sale. Her answer was wordless but eloquent: in typical Cretan fashion she raised her eyebrows and tilted her head back. Nothing! We didn't mind. We liked the mountains and their self-contained villages, but being near to the sea was important to us. As children, we had both lived at the coast and neither of us had ever lost our love of the seaside.

The next morning we returned to see the agent, following the distinctive scent of his aromatic pipe tobacco from pavement level up the stairs to his first-floor office. He rose from behind his desk, his head wreathed in light blue smoke. The warmth of his greeting suggested that he had something for us. "Good news!" he said. He had a client with an old house in a quiet village to the west where one could see the sea – after only a short drive. We felt a shudder of apprehension when he warned that the house would need some renovation... We hadn't yet experienced the full range and depth of Cretan estate agency euphemisms. Anyway, we could "view the property" the next day and with that in mind we decided to give home-seeking a miss until then. A former Prince of Wales, when asked what he had learned from all his official visits, replied: "Never pass up an opportunity to take a pee." Our Greek experiences had taught us never to miss a coffee break. Hania was bustling away all around us and we knew that we should sit down for a while before joining in. We took our coffee in a rather stylish café just across the road from the agent's office. It was definitely not the sort of place we would normally have chosen: all the staff had their hair in ponytails – even the women. Greek coffee cannot be made quickly or in an espresso machine and this place looked as if it had been built to sell frothy coffee to Haniotes in the fast lane of life. I was going to ask for a freshly-squeezed orange juice when, to my astonishment, amid all the café's modish chrome fittings I spotted the essential tools of the Greek coffee-maker's trade: a single-ring gas-cooker and the long-handled brass pot known as a *briki*. A purist had once told me that the gas ring itself was an abomination and the pot should be heated on a bed of glowing charcoal, but I was grateful enough that one could still buy a cup of coffee that hadn't been blown into existence. Real Greek coffee comes in a small cup if ordered as a single (*mono*) or a bigger cup if ordered as a double (*diplo*). Either way it should be sipped, not gulped, and it should always be accompanied by a glass of cold water. Only experience will tell you whether to order it sweet (*glyko*), medium (*metrio*) or sugarless (*sketo*). For northern Europeans, Greek coffee is an acquired taste, but once acquired its full, rich flavour is very difficult to relinquish. Our waiter brought us two excellent coffees and we sat and watched Hania go by. There were a lot of hair-buns and ponytails to be seen, mostly on Greek Orthodox monks and priests. These hairy clerics make their Anglican counterparts seem as smooth and bald as the curate's egg!

There's a lot to see in Hania and we did our best to keep going, but after the market, the cathedral and the archaeological museum, we needed our lunch... The red wine from the taverna barrel was too heavy for such a hot day and we had to return to Irini's for a siesta. Tourists don't generally do this, but it's a good idea. Many Haniotes also think it is and when in Hania it's good advice to do as they do – at least in this respect. It was six when we woke up, and Hania was starting up all over again. Although things are changing, a large part of the city still follows the traditional pattern of early start-afternoon snooze-late finish. Tourist shops don't shut, of course, but if you need a replacement double-reciprocating tappet-cock for your gizmo in mid-afternoon, you're done for! On the other hand, you can get one at half-past-eight in the evening. We had noticed a Chinese restaurant on the harbour front and wondered if Chinese food in Crete was the same as in England. It was. After our home-from-home dinner, we finished the day with a stroll along the seafront to an area called Nea Hora, where we took note of a number of promising-looking fish tavernas.

The next morning we followed the road out of Hania, the risen sun behind us. Although it was still quite early, tourists abounded and they were a traffic hazard. We passed kilometre after kilometre of swimsuited wobbly-botts and pot-bellies carelessly flip-flopping from one narrow pavement to another. Now and again some scantily-clad blondes would distract drivers, most of whom seemed strangely susceptible to the charms of pretty Scandinavians in thongs. It definitely paid to be vigilant while motoring on this road! We passed endless strings of car and bike rental agencies and shops displaying Euro-mountains of garishly-coloured inflatable "beach goods", leather-ware, pottery, and, for all I knew, "genuine" Arctic "Eskimo" mittens as well. Here and there, nightclubs and discos punctuated rows of tavernas and café-bars sporting multi-lingual menu-boards and the flags of all nations. The air was heavy with the smell of such traditional Greek fare as "deep-fried donuts". We felt certain that somewhere to be found there were candyfloss vendors, lettered-rock shops, tattoo-artists, fortune-tellers and amusement arcades. Every now and again we caught a glimpse of the sea to our right. At Platanias we decided to pull off the main road and see what horrors waited on the beach. To our astonishment, the sandy beach and the view from it was infinitely better than anything Margate or Blackpool could offer, even on those rare days when they didn't have clouds and rain. It seemed like a very good arrangement, stringing out most of the grott along the main road and leaving the beach as a haven.

After Platanias, the signs of heavy-duty tourism petered out, with just a few reminders dotted here and there along the main road. In the distance we could see the first of the island's two western promontories that jut out into the sea like two fingers raised towards northern Europe. We passed through Kolymbari, a nondescript place initially notable only for its perilous crossroads, and drove on towards our first "official" house-viewing.

The agent was waiting for us with the owner. Why does every silver lining have a cloud around it? The traditional stone house still had a roof and its big structural arches – a feature of old Cretan houses – were intact. There was even a *patateri*, the large stone trough used for treading grapes. The property looked good enough, inside and outside, but unfortunately it also had its downsides. It was in a nondescript hillside village with a grandstand view of the island's main east-west highway and the neighbouring house, which was a bit too close for our liking, had just been sold – to a foreign couple. "From Germany?" I asked. "From Essex," the seller unexpectedly replied. Our interest evaporated. Essen or Essex, it was all the same to us. We just didn't want to be living so close to "foreign" neighbours; and for all we knew, they might well feel the same. We told the agent that the house wasn't quite right for us. He explored this in his estate-agently way, trying to convince us that it was really exactly what we wanted, but our adamantine refusal to budge led him to accept defeat. "Maybe I will have something else for you if you would like to come to my office in a day or two," he said.

We decided to drive on towards Kastelli, the main town of far-western Crete. There was nothing much on the dozen kilometres of main road between Kolymbari and Kastelli, except for three large dogs, a goat and a donkey – all dead. The only other vehicles we saw were obvious MoT failures, smoking, rattling and weaving their way along. The edge of the highway was littered with boulders and large stones, which had tumbled from the crumbling, rocky slopes of olive tree-covered foothills. After passing a couple of petrol stations, some derelict buildings and a cement works, we came out of a bend, high up, and had a good view of a rubbish tip with the sea beyond. All Kastelli lay before us, hazy in the drifting smoke from a factory chimney. It was a singularly uninspiring sight. Just before the rubbish tip, the road itself had appeared to be parting company with the earth below. Was this the "blissful" west where we might find a new life? Somehow, we didn't think so…

CHAPTER THREE

The biggest surprise about Kastelli was the absence of donkeys. Not a single one was tethered outside any of the human watering holes along the main road. They would not have been out of place. Midday in Kastelli had something of the heavy, brooding feel of a frontier town in a western B-movie, except that it looked so run-down that any frontier must long since have moved elsewhere. The only clock we saw had stopped and the tumbleweed that should have been blowing around had obviously given up and put down roots again. Visitors arriving from the east were greeted by a derelict bus, with a roof-rack for crates of chickens and such like, a pile of mechanical junk and an ill-kept war memorial. Nothing said, "Welcome!" – except a bent and grimy sign. The town just petered out after a few minutes driving, and this despite obstructions by double-parked cars and huge kerbside wheely-bins overflowing with rubbish. Surely there was more to the place than this?

We turned around and drove back, parking outside a *kafeneon*, which turned out to be the "bus station". While we were there, a dilapidated green bus rattled in. It had a ladder going up onto its roof, where there was a rack – obviously for crates of chickens and such like! Surely the days of people travelling by bus with their baggage strapped to the roof had long since gone, even here? The central square was dominated by a statue of a seated Eleftherios Venizelos staring out over a tobacconist's kiosk. The monument had been sculpted by someone with an expat name, "McKnight". Perhaps this wasn't so odd; art knows no frontiers and, anyway, we're all Europeans now. There's probably a statue of Oliver Cromwell in Biggleswade knocked out by someone with a name like Iliakos Klimatismos. Taking their cue from Venizelos, about 30 unemployed itinerant workers lounged in the sunlit square, staring longingly at the tobacconist's kiosk. It was a depressing sight. We found more shops in a second street, which ran parallel to the main road. Kastelli was an untidy, flyblown place, shabby here, smarter there, but mostly scruffy, tired-looking and dusty. The narrow pavements were often blocked by cheap plastic chairs set out by the many *kafenea*. There were cars and trucks parked every which way. If this place was a resort, then so was Gravesend! Yet, Kastelli had a history. It was originally the port of the ancient city of Polyrinia. It became an important commercial centre during the Roman occupation of Crete and some ruins from this period were signposted, although the one we found looked more like a bombsite *circa* 1941. In the 16th Century, the Venetians rebuilt the town and gave it a large fortress – and its name. Later, the Turks came and knocked a few chips off Kastelli's block and then the Germans dropped in – by parachute… But that was all history-book stuff; now it was a quite different matter. Kastelli was virtually anonymous.

We decided against taking the guidebook's advice to stay a few nights to experience the town's "elusive charm" which, it warned, "one may have to dig deep to find". We agreed with the book: Kastelli town's charms were definitely elusive! Later, we came to realise that on this first visit we had missed the point: Kastelli's "charm" – its only charm – was that it was ordinary. It was extraordinary in that it had managed to remain ordinary! Susan remarked that a term like "unspoilt" was a rather difficult concept in Greece, where tourism might lead to a place becoming over-developed and losing its character, but Greek towns and villages in themselves could often grow to be hideously ugly, without any outside help, while remaining completely "unspoilt" as genuine communities in which newcomers would find friendship and good-neighbourliness. If appearances are what matter, then towns and villages in Tuscany and Provence will win, most times, but for human warmth, Greece heads the league of friendly nations.

We took our lunch in a taverna that made absolutely no concessions to the tourist trade. The proprietor ignored us for as long as he could and then approached us warily. This definitely wasn't because we looked foreign; he probably thought we were undercover tax inspectors. We had experienced this elsewhere in Greece. In the paranoid fantasy world of self-employed Greeks, The Tax Office is a secret police force with unlimited power to inflict physical and mental torture on its victims. Any unknown face is immediately suspect if there's a rumour that the inspectors are in the area. However, when he realised that we actually wanted lunch, he cheered up and recommended the sea bream that he had just bought from a fisherman-friend. The grilled fish was excellent – and inexpensive. After we had finished our meal, the proprietor brought a bottle of *tschikoudia* to the table and the three glasses in his hand showed that he intended to join us. He asked us what we were doing in Kastelli. We told him that we were thinking of moving, not to Kastelli – heaven forbid! – but to western Crete. We were baiting a hook: if you don't fish you definitely won't catch anything. "I thought you might be from the tax office!" he said and then quickly added, just in case we were, "Not that I've got anything to worry about, of course…" He told us that he had heard of a house for sale in a "pretty" village nearby, but before we could get any details out of him he launched off into an account of his own problems, which were overwhelmingly financial and which the profit on our meal wasn't going to do anything to relieve. He brought his story to an end by dramatically thrusting his open hand, palm first, into his face and bitterly saying, *"Faskelono ta moutra mou!"* (I showed myself my hand!) This was a personal insult – to himself. The most offensive gesture in Greece is the emphatic forward thrust of the open hand with the fingers spread out. It doesn't mean, "Stop!"; it's more a sort of "up your's!" – but one-and-a-half times worse, being five fingers against our usual two. We expressed our sympathy and I found myself nervously sitting on my hands lest in an unguarded moment I gestured something I really didn't mean to say. We steered the conversation back to our problem, but all we got was more body language, this time the increasingly familiar backward tilt of the head. He knew nothing. We paid the bill and decided to go for coffee to see if anyone in Kastelli knew about houses for sale in "pretty" villages.

Two coffees later we were talking to a man who had a friend who had a house for sale. When we said we would like to find out more, he left us, returning a few minutes later, friend-less, but with the information that the house on offer was big and had a good garden – distinguished by a large lemon tree – and truly magnificent views. Or so his friend had told him... He said we could speak to his friend later. When we explained that we were staying in Hania and couldn't just wait around, he offered to make some arrangements for us; he told us to telephone him in the evening.

The house was in the village of Drapanias. There are two roads from Kastelli to Kolymbari, the old and the new. We had arrived by the new and now we decided to return via the old, stopping in Drapanias to see if we liked the place. The old road was a joy to travel. The new road had taken away its traffic and it was very quiet. On either side there were mostly olive groves, edged with a rich variety of greenery: there were eucalyptus, fig, mulberry, palm, almond and cypress trees and others we didn't know. There were dense banks of bamboo and *skinos* – the local version of the English lentisk – with bursts of glorious colour from oleanders, mallow and geraniums, which seem to be always in flower in Crete. There were prickly pears and other things we could only have identified with a botanical guide.

Just before Drapanias we saw a sign pointing to the "Villa Trevizan". The guidebook said nothing about it. Perhaps it was a hotel? We decided to take a look. We found it to be the melancholy ruin of an old house, probably a villa from Venetian times. It had an "Italian" feel about it at any rate. The building looked as if it was deteriorating rapidly. A coat-of-arms, all detail eroded by time and the elements, sat high up above the open front door. The rambling building was mostly roofless and pigeons sat on the skeletal rafters. Fig trees sprouted from the earth floor, which was littered with bits of rusting junk and droppings from the cooing birds above. At the foot of an external stone staircase someone had dumped an old gearbox. There was no one around to ask about the house, although close-by, and somewhat incongruous against such a setting, was a raw-looking new house sporting a satellite-dish.

The village was just up the road a little, beyond the "illuminations", which were strung across the road and wished everyone, "A Happy New Year". It was now summer... Drapanias turned out to be a friendly village of picturesque ruination, with crooked alleyways and flowers everywhere. The villagers were obviously keen gardeners. The village had a rural smell; there were certainly plenty of animals around, from splendid peacocks, free-ranging chickens, ducks, rabbits, cats-a-plenty and dogs, including a very strange little one with elephantine ears and dachshund legs. We stopped to talk to a goat and her kid because we knew from experience that it was one way of finding out about houses for sale! No such luck this time, but the halt brought us face to face with a memorial on the wall of a nearby building:

HERE WERE MURDERED
ON 23 MAY 1941
EMMANUEL M. NIKOLAKAKIS
TEACHER AGED 20
AND
EVANGELOS S. SKOULAKIS
AGED 19
BY THE BARBARIC GERMANS

Large public war memorials are one thing, but allowing this brutally honest little memento to remain looked like an oversight. Cretans generally appear to have opted for a "don't mention the war" policy; in fact, the Turks, who left in 1898, are still seen as infinitely worse than the Germans! The details of the savage nazi occupation of the island from 1941-45 are now mostly buried away as part of the history of a previous century, even though the events are still well within living memory for many Cretans. It's an approach that has paid off because every summer hordes of jolly Germans now wallow on the beaches, untroubled by embarrassing reminders of the dreadful atrocities committed by their forebears in nearby villages. The truth is that there's no profit of any kind to be had from rubbing German noses in the dirt of their nation's appalling past – even if you could. The Cretans themselves are even-handed in their dealings with their former enemies and allies: German excesses and the allied sacrifice of 3,579 men listed as killed or missing in the shambolic defence of the island in 1941 appear to be equally forgotten.

Walking around Drapanias we found a beautiful site with a truly spectacular view over the Bay of Kissamos. From such a place it would be a joy every evening to watch the sun disappear. The building was in poor condition, but attractive and redeemable, and it had a lush garden with a big lemon tree. Could this be it? We each confessed to our excitement, which was only slightly dimmed by the sound of traffic from the distant but visible main road. We walked further only to find that lots of houses had gardens with big lemon trees. Then we came across a tumbledown, derelict pile, housing chickens who had no view whatsoever, although if they flew up on to the roof they might get one. This house had a big, big lemon tree. We tried to convince ourselves that it wasn't *that* big, but the edge had gone from our excitement. We consoled ourselves with the thought that it was no use guessing, we'd have to wait until we could talk to the seller.

On our way back to the car, we came across a cheerful old lady, dressed in black and sitting outside her whitewashed house. She was a picture, framed on three sides by bushes of white, red and pink geraniums. We exchanged greetings and pleasantries and she invited us into her house for a drink. We squeezed into a tiny room and she sat on her ancient bed while we took two traditional rush-bottomed chairs. We chatted for a while and then the telephone rang. It was her daughter, who had long since moved away from the village. When the daughter heard that her mother was entertaining strangers – and foreigners at that – she apparently said: "In the house! They will rob you – or worse!" The old lady just said, "Silly woman!" and put the 'phone down, preferring to chat to us. We told her about our house-hunting and she said we could have her place when they took her off to "the cypress trees", which is a Cretan euphemism for the cemetery. She was pensive for a few seconds – we thought she was contemplating her mortality – but then she said, "No, my daughter would kick up a fuss!" We thanked her for the thought and promised that we would visit again.

We rejoined the old road and continued our drive back to Hania, but not for long. My eye was caught by a bright new yellow, brown and white sign: "Ancient Minoan and Classic Settlement."

We followed the sign down a bumpy dirt road across an olive grove. There were olive trees and more olive trees, but no ancient site. Then we could go no further; the track was blocked by a monstrous greenhouse of battered, yellowing plastic sheeting bulging with tomatoes. There was still no sign of an ancient site, unless the greenhouse qualified. I had just turned the car around, with difficulty, when the tomato-grower arrived on a stuttering moped. *"Yassas"*, he smiled and disappeared behind his cracked and lumpy plastic sheeting. If this had been England he would have stared at us and pointedly asked, "Can I help you?" We got out of the car and stood there nonplussed. He emerged from his tomatoes, smiled another *"Yassas"* at us, and mounted his moped. "Excuse me," I said. "Could you tell us where the Ancient Minoan and Classic Settlement is?" Now it was his turn to look nonplussed. "The what?" he asked. I explained that we had followed a sign – a brand new sign – from the main road and that there was supposed to be an ancient settlement around here somewhere. "Ah, yes," he said. "They put that sign there for the tourists." I said that was understandable but where was the ancient settlement that the tourists were supposed to look at? "Well," he said, lowering his voice as if taking us into his confidence, "there was one – but that was a long time ago." His moped spluttered into life and stuttered its way back through the olive trees to the main road. We looked at each other and simultaneously repeated, "There was one – but that was a long time ago…"

The menu board of a taverna at the outskirts of Drapanias had boldly offered "Atmosphere", apparently at no extra charge. The tourist attractions of the village and its environs were obviously a bit thin on the ground – and some, like the sign-posted ancient settlement, weren't even to be found on the ground; others looked as if they might soon fall to the ground! Perhaps "atmosphere" was all that Drapanias had to offer but that was, after all, what we were really looking for; at least in its genuine form and not just as so much hot air. We had said often enough that we did not want to live anywhere that could be described as "a popular tourist location" and so we carried on back to Hania to telephone a man about a house.

The old road was a delight all the way back to Kolymbari. It had climbed from Drapanias towards Plakalonas, from where there was a breath-taking panoramic view of sea and mountains, which, in England, would definitely have been turned into an official viewpoint, with benches and "visitor facilities". Here it was just as nature had left it. Hamlets and churches dotted the surrounding hillsides but there was very little along the road itself, just a few houses and a number of "primitive" wayside shrines, in which we had always taken an interest. There was also the common Greek blight of occasional fly-tips of rubbish: car seats, cookers, refrigerators, mattresses, sacks, plastic containers, bits of rotten furniture – it was all there, amid the blossoming oleanders! Every now and again the road showed signs of subsiding, but it remained an appealing route, green and cool. The car windows were open and even above the noise of the engine we could hear the chirping chatter of the cicadas and smell the scent of the abundant wild fennel.

Back in Hania we found a telephone and two calls later were speaking to the man from Drapanias. He described his house in glowing terms and when we asked for more details it turned out that it was obviously the tumbledown pile with the chickens in it. He wanted 20 million drachmas – about 15 million more than we would be prepared to pay even if it had been in much better condition and in a better position. He pooh-poohed our objections to the price and told us we could build a hotel there to which tourists would flock and we'd become rich! We told him we didn't think so; he invited us to "think about it" because Cretans can never take no for an answer.

Downcast, we went for a walk in the streets behind Hania's old harbour. We made a tout happy and accepted his invitation to "dine with me tonight". Apart from the possibilities that the tout had a hypnotic personality or that a feeling of depression had lowered our resistance, we could find no explanation for our bizarre submission to his blandishments. The menu was a tasselled affair in five languages, including broken English, and more dishes than the number of tables could need or justify; there were even a dozen different fancy ice creams, all illustrated! The ping-ping-ping of microwaves was audible even above the too-loud mock-Cretan piped music. The food was served far too hot and in severely controlled portions, which was probably to everyone's benefit because it was only just on the Plimsoll line of edibility. Indeed, the pork-and-peppers dish that I had chosen had a very close affinity to plimsolls! The bread was dry, the salt-cellar empty and the toothpicks looked secondhand. If the wine was from a barrel it was from a plastic one kept well above room temperature. Our waiter was very jolly but we suspected his constant laughter represented a joke at our expense. All of the customers seemed to be first-timers – and probably last-timers, too. We reckoned that we would not be alone in deciding against repeating the experience.

We ended the day with the consoling thought that in the morning we would be visiting the estate agent again and that perhaps he would have something for us... We realised then that we were beginning to fall in love with western Crete. Hania was a Venetian-Turkish delight for short-stay visitors; Kastelli was a dump, period. Between the two we had caught a glimpse of an idiosyncratic world we felt that we would like to know more of. It was eccentric, whimsical, lush – and, wonder of wonders, "blissfully free of the crowds and commercialism". We decided that we weren't really depressed at all!

CHAPTER FOUR

The next morning saw us heading for a village on the western side of the Rodopou peninsula, between Kolymbari and Kastelli. The agent had come up with something: his grandfather's old house. He was very relaxed about it; in fact, his sales pitch was modest. The house needed working on but if we liked it we could have it for just 1,000,000 drachmas. This was more like it! We were to go to the village, find one of his relatives and give them a business card, on the back of which had been jotted a request for someone to show us the house. The relative was easily found and the three of us walked up the main village street, past a donkey tethered alongside an abandoned Ford Cortina, to a dilapidated stone-and-rubble house built into the side of a hill. It was semi-detached, which immediately put us off because the way some of these old houses are built means that you will always be dependent upon your neighbour for the structural integrity of your own home. We wanted to live here because we liked the place and the people, but that's not the same as saying that we liked *everything*. My father, who was a Brummie, always used to call his hammer "the Birmingham screwdriver"; Greeks like to think of the bulldozer as an instrument to be used for fine-tuning! To us, semi-detached meant totally risky. We could see the possibilities in the house, even through the mess made by the chickens who normally inhabited it, but it wasn't what we wanted.

Further up the road we came across an old ruin with a sign on it. Greek stationery shops sell ready-printed signs proclaiming either *POLEITAI*, literally "it is for sale", or *ENOIKIAZETAI*, if it is to let. This one was a *POLEITAI* sign and gave a telephone number. We were looking at the building, without much enthusiasm, when a woman stopped and asked us if we would like to look at a house that she wanted to sell. We walked with her to an unremarkable old building, but it was off the road, attractively surrounded by greenery and definitely in better condition than the other two on offer. We were invited back to her own house for coffee, over which she revealed that she knew we had been shown the agent's grandfather's former home. This didn't surprise us. It is very difficult to do anything in a Greek village without it being public knowledge. That's probably why marital fidelity is still so strong a habit! The woman was hungry for details. Greek conversation owes more to darts than to cricket; if someone wants to know something, they go straight for the bull rather than spin-bowl you an indirect question. "What was the price of the house you went to look at?" she asked. We told her: 1,000,000 drachmas. She was flabbergasted – and she wasn't acting. She was obviously one of those Cretans who thought that every heap of rubble was really a crock of gold, provided, of course, that you could find a daft foreigner to sell it to. As soon as we told her that we thought 1,000,000 was about right, her interest in us began to wane; it was obvious that we weren't the kind of daft foreigners she'd heard about. We easily made our excuses and left.

We said farewell to the village, which, by the standards of Drapanias, had been a dull place and hadn't struck any chords within us. We decided to explore further by returning to Kolymbari and driving back along the old road towards Kastelli, taking the first turning that we came to. It was a right-hand turn, sign-posted for Rodopou. An old peasant woman walking on the road waved to us and because we all seemed to be in the middle of nowhere in particular we stopped and asked her if she would like a lift. "To the top of the hill," she said. At the top of the hill I stopped and the old woman got out of the car and presented us with a bouquet of what looked like weeds. This was freshly-picked *horta*, the very tasty and nutritious "greens" traditionally gathered wild from the mountainsides in winter by Cretan peasants – men and women – who know exactly where to look and what to look for, and cultivated all over the place in summer. Well, that was our dinner sorted out! We waved farewell and drove on, deciding that we would take another turning to see what that might lead to. Perhaps a main course of rabbit or chicken! We came to a crossroads; straight ahead and left was asphalted, while to the right there was a rutted track.

We stopped the car and got out to admire the scenery. It was verdant. Tree-covered hills receded into distant mountains. Between the lower hills stood sentinel columns of dark cypress trees. It was blissfully quiet. No artist's impression could have rendered this landscape more serene. I had always believed in serendipity, that happy knack of accidentally making unexpected yet delightful discoveries. This was pure serendipity! I turned to Susan and said, "You know, I think we could live here..." The discordant braying of a not-too-distant donkey interrupted my reverie – but the magic stayed. Susan agreed; it was what she had had in her mind's eye when we first talked about living in Greece.

Back in the car, we decided to head in the direction of the noisy donkey. We took the rutted track, which led us up to Aspra Nera, where we stopped to look at the village. We didn't get a rabbit or a chicken in Aspra Nera but we did drink *tschikoudia*. We met a quiet, dignified man leading his donkey down a track. He stopped and greeted us with a courtly little bow. In answer to his questions, we told him where we came from and gave him our names. He responded by introducing himself. "I am Aristoteles," he said and then, tapping his forehead, added, "but I am no philosopher!" He invited us to visit his house, where we sat for a while with glasses of *tschikoudia* while he told us about his life. He had been in the merchant navy and had seen something of the world but now he was happy in sleepy little Aspra Nera, with his wife and family, his animals and his fields. His philosophy sounded fine to me! We met his son and two teenage daughters who greeted us warmly and showed none of the gaucherie that many of their English contemporaries would have displayed in the same situation. The six of us sat and chatted for a while but we didn't try to steer the conversation around to house-hunting because delightful though Aristoteles' village was, it was only a hamlet – truly a one-donkey place!

The next village along the unmade road was Astratigos, which was behind us before we realised we had been in it. We would have turned back but the road ahead looked more inviting. We stopped to admire the scene. The road was high up and the sea could be seen as the backdrop to a landscape both green and rocky. A bird of prey circled slowly in the clear blue sky ahead of us. I turned to Susan: "I really do like this," I said. She did too. We drove on and came to a halt in Afrata.

We wandered through the village, which was not particularly attractive in itself, although it was made more appealing by the abundance of flowers, with hibiscus, Bougainvillaea and geraniums everywhere. It looked as if there might be an "Afrata in Bloom" competition under way, with the two *kafenea* by the village square – the Asteri ("The Star") and the Kali Kardia ("The Good Heart") – competing with each other for first prize. We tossed a 100-drachma coin; heads – in this case, that of Alexander the Great – we would eat at the Asteri. It was tails, so we stopped for a snack at the Kali Kardia. After an alfresco lunch of fried eggs and chips, we explored further and found a picturesque old footpath, which meandered past old houses – and yet more geranium bushes – down towards the church. It was sad to think that the entire village had probably looked like this before its "modernisers" got to work. We thought that Afrata might be a very good example of a spoilt-yet-unspoilt Cretan village.

At the outskirts of the village, sandwiched between the church and a sheep pen, sat the cemetery. I jumped up on to a concrete slab to get a better view of our surroundings and, looking down, saw a skull staring up at me. I was standing on an ossuary, which someone had left uncovered. One false step and I might have found myself in the middle of a heap of human bones. The church was locked so we walked out of the village a little way, turning to look back at the view for visitors approaching directly from Kolymbari. The backdrop to the village was a vast wall of scrub-dotted mountain, the ridge of which was the spine of the Rodopou peninsula. It was a dramatic sight. The village, the most northerly inhabited point on the peninsula, sat at the foot of this great wall. Following the spine would have taken one way out into the Mediterranean and, eventually, at the tip of the peninsula, to the site of the ancient settlement of Diktyna. The archaeologists said that people had been living around Afrata for 20,000 years. We weren't surprised. The red earth was obviously fertile and the village was close to the sea. Its location was spectacular, with splendid views of distant mountain ranges. Another bonus was the climate, which was much kinder than places lower down; Afrata was about 150 metres above sea level and enjoyed a gentle breeze, which would make even the hottest days bearable.

We decided to walk a little way up the mountain. Just outside the village, I stopped to look back at a small single-storey stone building all on its own amid the olive trees. Its position gave it a fine view of the sea and of the distant peaks of the White Mountains range. I told Susan that that was exactly where I'd like to be able to have a house. She agreed. We rambled on along a rugged track obviously used mostly by sheep and goats. We were high up and were enjoying splendid views to Hania and beyond when I decided to make use of a large boulder just ahead. My hand had just reached my zipper when I heard Susan suddenly  speak in Greek. I stopped. There, sitting completely camouflaged against the boulder, was a shepherd. He was not very tall, his wide smile was almost toothless and his eyes twinkled with good humour. His grizzled hair and moustache and weather-beaten face suggested that he was quite elderly but he exuded an impish quality which belied that. He was dressed in the style of a wartime partisan. He had traditional muddy-green jodhpur-type baggy breeches, which British troops had nicknamed "crap-catchers", and scuffed knee-high leather boots. He had been sitting in the lee of the boulder, the bent *skinos* tree above his head showing the direction in which the wind usually blew. We chatted while he continued to watch his flock grazing the scrubby mountainside. "I don't see many tourists up here," he said, his chuckle showing that he was undoubtedly overstating the fact. He seemed genuinely pleased that we were from England and told us how during the war he had thwarted the Germans by hiding two allied soldiers in a cave high up on the mountain that towered above us. He then told us about his dreadful wartime experiences in Albania, when frostbite had nearly cost him his toes, and how a German bomb had later left him with a lifelong ear problem. We couldn't equal any of this, but we chatted along. We were obviously getting on well so we asked him if he knew of any houses for sale in this part of the island. He mused on this and then stood up and said, "My friend has a house to sell. I would introduce you but I can't leave the sheep yet. Come and visit me tomorrow morning. You can't miss my house in the village – it's got a big lemon tree in the garden." We laughed and he looked at us quizzically. We didn't try to explain. He told us his name, but we only caught the first part, Yiannis, because at that moment a nearby sheep chose to choke on a fig leaf, drowning out the rest of what was said.

Back in the village, we stopped at the other *kafeneon*, the Asteri. The Asteri's proprietress was a sweet-looking little old lady dressed rather like an English nun. She served us coffee and sat down for a chat. Now full of the spirit of nothing-ventured-nothing-gained, we told her that we were house-hunting. She casually informed us that her family was selling the old village olive mill and its attached house with a big garden – which apparently had almond trees, but no lemons. Afrata was proving to be a most unusual place. She told us we could look at the property if we wanted to, not tomorrow but immediately! She pointed it out to us and left us to look around on our own. It was an old stone-built property of advanced ruination with definitely more character than substance, but full of possibilities and in a quiet lane just off the centre of the village. The ancient olive-press, which had been made in Turkey, was still intact and there were several huge millstones. We went back to the *kafeneon* and asked the price. Five million drachmas for the lot. We knew that restoration would prove to be a major, lengthy and costly undertaking – and a Turkish olive press definitely wasn't on our list of desired antiques – but we said we would think about it.

We set off back to Irini's. Our *horta* was now a little limp but we couldn't look this gift horse in the mouth. We planned to go straight to the *agora* – the public market – in Hania and buy some traditional local cheese, *mizithra*, which is made from either goat's milk or, better still, from sheep's, some olives, bread and whatever else took our fancy, so that we could make our own dinner. The way down to Kolymbari from Afrata wound through olive groves, vineyards and pasture land. A right-hand bend in the road suddenly brought the broad expanse of the Cretan Sea into view and then a wall of scrub-dotted mountainside appeared in the distance. A short stretch of crash barrier protected drivers from a fatal plunge onto the rocky shoreline far below. Along the road, sheep and goats grazed careless of passing cars. Several hairpin bends further on we had descended far enough to hear the sea. We passed a little bay from which someone was swimming and then the road became like a ledge cut into the edge of the mountain, with a wall of rock on one side and the sea on the other. Clumps of pink oleander grew where they could. We passed a beautifully situated but hideously ugly wayside shrine and then, without any warning, hit a blind bend under an overhanging rock. Fortunately, it was a very quiet road. The towers of the tranquil-looking Monastery of Gonia came into view, blighted, but only slightly, by the nearby modern buildings of an international study and conference centre. Just before reaching the monastery there was a pretty, heavily-wooded little bay, this one with three swimmers! The last stretch of road took us down a long avenue of tamarisk and pine trees, their trunks painted white, past Kolymbari's small harbour and into the village's high street which led directly to the poorly-marked crossroads where a left-turn would take us on to the main highway directly back to Hania – or a collision with something if we weren't careful.

The following morning, the road up to Afrata seemed different. There was an even greater sensation of openness, probably because there was no cliff wall to hug. The sea was just down there, below Susan's right elbow. For most of its length, absolutely nothing stood between the edge of the road and the rocky shore far below. It was a steep climb back up to the village. The peninsula stretched out before us and in the distance a large cave could be seen like a black hole in the cliff face. The last major bend now swung to our left and ahead of us was Afrata's distinctive backdrop – the wall of mountain. At the outskirts of the village we passed two dogs, chained to large and rusty oil-drum "kennels", and apparently mounting guard. They ignored us as we drove past into the village. We parked on Afrata's scruffy central square, which sported a lot of weeds and the bare concrete base of an unfinished memorial.

We started to look for a house with a big lemon tree, although, by now, experience should have taught us better. There were, of course, lots of lemon trees. We stopped a villager and asked him if he knew a shepherd called Yiannis. This was a bit like asking someone in the Rhondda Valley if they'd ever known a coal-miner called Evans! We described Yiannis and the villager's eyes lit up with recognition. "Ah," he said, "you want Dagounoyianni!" Did we? We didn't think this was the name we'd half-heard. Later we discovered that names were another Cretan peculiarity. We were looking for Yiannis Dagounakis, but in the village there were so many men called Yiannis that they had had to find a way of allowing each one to keep his name and his individuality. They did this by taking half of the surname and tacking it on the front of the Christian name. Hence, "Dagounoyianni". Junking the suffix -*akis* from their names wasn't a difficult thing for them to do. According to legend, it was imposed by the occupying Turks as a psychological manoeuvre to put the Cretans down. It is a diminutive; thus, parents with a son called *Antonis*, will call him *Antonakis* – "little Anthony" – which is actually what Yiannis eventually took to calling me! The other side of this legend is that after the Turks were defeated and relinquished their control of the island, the Cretans kept up the Turkish "name-calling" as if to say, "Oh, yes! And who are the 'little people' now?" The only part of Crete where you don't find the -*akis* suffix so often is Sfakia, on the south coast, where the locals claim that they were the ones doing the name-calling.

Yiannis was still up on the mountainside when we found his house but his wife, Dimitra, was waiting for us. She gave us a warm welcome, told us she had expected us earlier and said lunch wouldn't be long. Lunch? It was only 10.45! Yiannis turned up and said his friend had asked him to show us the house if we were still interested. We said that we were very keen to see it, impatient

47

even. Despite that, he insisted that we had lunch before anything else. We weren't in the slightest bit hungry but what could we do? Lunch was a challenge: it was boiled – and fatty – mutton. I sneaked a glance at my watch; it was coffee time. The last person to serve me food like this was a school dinner lady, 40 years ago. Then there was an easy way of dealing with the problem: toss it behind a radiator or dump it on someone else's plate! Here there was no way out but to swallow hard. Or so I thought... Susan, who had confessed to feeling a bit off-colour before we had set out, leaned across and dropped a lump of sinewy gristle on my plate. "You'll like that bit," she said affectionately in Greek and then added forcefully in English, "...and, please, I don't want it back!" Dimitra, obviously mortified to think that I hadn't been given enough of what I really wanted, fished about in the pot, found an even bigger lump of the same sinewy gristle and added it to my plate. I looked across at Yiannis, a bone in his hands, sucking away at it as if it was the most delicious thing in the world. To him, of course, it was; to me it was a torture. I knew that by any measure this was good food, but it just wasn't to my taste. Slowly, like a sparrow, I picked at little bits of meat. My suffering was eased by a pile of home-made bread and a decanter of red wine. After the first two glasses, Yiannis stopped pouring and told me to help myself. I was proceeding at the rate of one glass of wine to every forkful of mutton, which emptied the decanter rather quickly. Yiannis dismissed my apologies, jerking his thumb to the back of the kitchen where there sat an ancient 1,000-litre wooden barrel. "There's plenty still in there," he laughed as he got up to refill the decanter. Between pecking and drinking I made a respectable enough impression on the meat to be allowed off eating any more. I finished my lunch at 11.45, barely sober.

At the table, Yiannis had talked about the literature of Nikos Kazantzakis, the author of *Zorba the Greek*. It seemed an unlikely topic for a shepherd but the better we got to know Yiannis the more we recognised that he was an unusual individual with wide-ranging interests in literature, history and politics, particularly politics. Dimitra, like most village women, was more interested in our family, especially our children. She asked us how many we had and when we told her seven – between us – we saw our stock rise with her. Yiannis seemed to be settling down for a long discourse on British foreign policy in the late 1940s – a subject about which we knew absolutely nothing – and so we thought we should remind him of the reason for our visit. "Of course," he said. "Let's go."

The three of us left the house, climbed up a delightful old footpath, past flowers and trees, crossed a patch of rough grazing land and found ourselves on a farm track. We had only walked along the track a short distance when the little stone building that I had seen the day before came into view. Yiannis walked us through a gap in a dry-stone boundary wall and up to its doorway, from which the door itself had long since gone. We stood in a window-less single room with an earth floor, at least I assumed it was earth, but we definitely weren't inside a house. It was more like a stable! Yiannis chuckled and said, "Of course, it needs a bit of work..." He paused and then suggested that we take a really good look around outside. The building was irrelevant; Yiannis knew that and we were to realise it soon enough. We stepped outside, into the sunlight, and saw a patchwork Mediterranean landscape of dry-stone walls, olive groves and vineyards. The little building had its back towards a towering wall of scrub-covered mountain, on which sheep were grazing, while on the other three sides were views of more-distant mountains – including the majestic peaks of the Lefka Ori – and the sea, which sparkled beneath an Olympic blue sky. There were no houses close by and the agricultural track came to an end at the corner of this plot. The site was small but the location perfect. We wandered away from Yiannis, who appeared to be admiring the floor of the stable. It didn't take us long to decide that although the site was small, very small, it was big enough for a house for the two of us. We had no fixed ideas about the kind of house we wanted and we were quite prepared to build a new one, possibly incorporating the stable into it. The experience of restoring our "antique" cottage in Kent had taught us that new houses were not without their merits. There's more to life than spending the weekends studying ancient chimney pots through binoculars or poking sticks down blocked drains. Behind the stable was an uncultivated field. I asked Yiannis if he knew anything about it. "It would make a fine garden for this place," was all he said.

We returned to Yiannis's house where we discussed the site. Yiannis pointed out that the track to the site was the only way one could approach by car and it was in bad condition. That suited us; it would keep Sunday drivers away. The only other way to the site was on foot, uphill all the way from the village. "No problem," we told him. He telephoned his friend on our behalf and it was agreed that we would all meet at Yiannis's at 7 o'clock the following evening. It was now time for Yiannis's afternoon nap and so we left him. We walked back up to the site to take another look. We climbed up onto the roof of the stable and drank in the views. Yes, we would buy it – unless, heaven forbid, the owner had already decided that we were daft foreigners waiting to be fleeced. Hanging in the old fig tree outside the stable door I found a shepherd's crook. Was this a bad omen?

CHAPTER FIVE

In our heads, we already owned the stable, but while hoping for the best we also thought we should prepare for the worst. We left Hania early and drove towards Kolymbari, planning to explore other villages in the area before negotiations began in the evening. Susan had got the telephone number of an estate agent who was supposed to know about houses for sale in the west. Our experience with the first agent had reinforced our reluctance to have anything to do with this one, who, according to Susan's informant – the baker from whom we bought fresh bread every morning – was also a "foreigner". However, because we had time on our hands – and, of course, "You never know, he might just have something..." – we used a roadside 'phone to call him. He said we could find him in a bar just off the main road. The description he gave of himself wasn't very flattering and so we felt better about seeing him. If he could describe himself like that, he was unlikely to exaggerate the charms of any houses on his books! His "books" turned out to be a grubby school exercise book kept in a battered briefcase alongside a well-chewed ballpoint pen. In truth, he wasn't absolutely certain about very much in that book of his but he was eager to try to be of service. He offered to plaster Afrata and Kolymbari with notices saying "Houses and land wanted for foreign buyers". We were horrified. We told him, very firmly, not to bother on our behalf. If he had put up those notices, property prices would have rocketed and probably stayed in orbit for years.

After that narrow escape, lunchtime loomed. The village in which we stopped couldn't offer any food and the only thing that delayed us getting back in the car and driving straight on was the sight of a blisteringly-white house, which looked as if it had been pat-a-caked together from icing sugar and lard. My first guess was that it was a DIY job by someone who shouldn't have. It was obviously an old building which had had a new face plastered over it. Everything about it was raw, crude and out of kilter. It wasn't at all eccentric; it was just plain ugly – the work of a botcher. An English voice suddenly boomed out: "Ha! Hello there!" We looked up. There, leaning out of an upper window, was the source of the voice. "Are you English?" he asked. We hesitantly confessed that we were. "Good," he said, "half-a-mo..." The front door opened before we could turn and flee.

We accepted his invitation to have a drink because we thought he might be helpful and informative. He wasn't, except by default. He showed us around the house, which appeared to have been clumsily cobbled together without any considerations of convenience, comfort or appearance, pointing out various defects and mocking each one as he did so. It was a guided tour of a fine example of jerry-building. Was the owner the cowboy builder responsible for the mess? Not knowing made it difficult to respond to his commentary with anything but inarticulate grunts. In the end, he put us on the spot: "What do your goodselves think of it, then?" I wanted to say, "It's crap!" – but of course I didn't. I lied and told him that I thought it was a house of character. "Count yourselves lucky you don't know the 'character' responsible!" snapped our guide's wife, who had appeared without warning or introduction. Did she mean her husband? It seemed possible.... The glum silence that followed was broken by Susan: "Did you employ someone...?" This kick-started our host back into confessional chattering mode. It was a depressing tale. They had engaged an agent to act for them, but despite fulsome promises that they would get the best deals going, they paid far too much for the house and for the botched building work. They were overcharged for poor materials and the work was given to a gang of unskilled day-labourers, who did what they were told, more or less, and probably did it as well as they could, which, in this case, meant very badly. There had been no proper contract, planning or supervision and I didn't hold out much hope for the owner's proposed "action" against his agent, unless he was planning to hire an assassin and start a Cretan blood feud!

Susan obviously thought that the couple had hung their brains on the coat-rack; my initial sympathy was dented by the owner's final words on the subject: "Don't you worry we'll not get caught again! You know, we had to get a plumber in to put some things right for us. He seemed a nice enough bloke and afterwards he invited us to his house for a meal. I thought I'd have a look at *his* bathroom while I was there, and do you know, he had gold-plated taps. A Cretan plumber with gold-plated taps! I reckoned I'd paid for them with what he charged me, the bugger! After that I got someone back home to find me tradesmen and I brought them out here from England. Yes I did! I paid the airfares and everything. And I'll do it again! Hang the expense! I'm not going to be ripped off by foreigners!" he shouted.

This perverse xenophobia was our cue for departure, but when we said that we had to get going they pleaded with us to stay for lunch. Despite all the bluster, they looked a rather pathetic pair – and there was no doubt that they had been very cruelly ripped off. Maybe it was their own fault, but we couldn't help feeling sorry for them. We agreed to stay, but it was a mistake and afterwards we felt sorry for ourselves. Our host was very coy about what he had done in England but from the way he barbecued I suspected that he had operated a waste incinerator. After well-charred chump chops, soggy chips and a glutinous aubergine porridge-like dip we felt we really had to leave. We declined the offer of instant coffee and slowly extricated ourselves from this depressing encounter. "Come again," we were told.

In the car, I asked Susan what the woman had talked about when they were together in the kitchen. "Well, she told me that she couldn't buy blancmange locally and had to have it sent out from England." My conversation had been equally bizarre: "He asked me if I'd ever seen the film *Basic Instinct*. That's the one in which Sharon Stone sits down, crosses her legs and is supposed to reveal that she's sans knickers. He said the film had been on TV the previous night but he hadn't been able to see a thing because of the Greek sub-titles plastered right across her lap!" "What a wally!" said Susan.

We still had about four hours to kill until our rendezvous at Yiannis's house. We wanted to take another look at Afrata but we didn't want to be spotted hanging around there so we decided to drive across to the ancient site of Polyrinia, a few kilometres south of Kastelli. Halfway there we stopped for coffee, although I would have preferred a refreshing glass of Andrews Liver Salts. We stopped at a small *kafeneon* and went inside to find the proprietor sitting there with a heavily-bandaged foot stuck up in the air. Coffee was out of the question; he couldn't move, not since yesterday when he had dropped a rock on his foot. "Accidentally," he pointed out. We said we were sorry to hear it, wished him a speedy recovery and turned to leave. "Of course," he said, "you could do it for yourselves…" I assured him that I knew how to make Greek coffee and he waved me behind the counter. I was now a *kafeneon*-keeper! I had prepared everything for two coffees when, obviously satisfied that I did know what I was doing, he asked me to make him a cup as well. The three of us sat and drank our coffee together. Another customer came in and I prepared to return to my gas ring but, disappointingly, he wanted a bottle of beer. When we came to leave our offer to pay was firmly refused. We found our way to Polyrinia. It was a jumble of ruins in a beautiful site but we did not do it justice because our minds kept turning to our own little ruin and the meeting ahead.

Kryiacos Platsakis, a stout, elderly and moustachioed man with a touch of the old Cretan bandit chief (retired!) about him, was waiting for us at Yiannis's house with his son, Aristides, the local metalworker. We chatted inconsequentially around Dimitra's kitchen table for half-an-hour, *tschikoudia* lubricating the wheels

of our new acquaintanceship, and then Yiannis coughed significantly. This was a signal for all of us to get on with the negotiations. We asked about the land and Kyriacos told us it had belonged to his mother. He had built the stable for his mule, Turnip, back in 1950 from old stones salvaged from restoration work at the local church, carting each of them on his back uphill along the rugged footpath to the site. Why was he selling? The money was more useful than a tiny plot of land on the outskirts of the village and anyway it was years since they'd had a mule or a donkey – and they had no intention of getting another because the family vehicle was now a four-wheel-drive Toyota! The family owned a lot of land in the village; the piece under discussion might be important to us but it wasn't to them.

Yiannis had primed us on the etiquette of the occasion. Kyriacos would – eventually – state his price and we would be *expected* to make a counter-offer. Apparently no one should ever pay the asking price for a piece of Cretan land! That's something that only daft foreigners do and we were determined not to be seen as having more money than sense. We had asked Yiannis if a much lower figure from us would cause offence. He had laughed and said that of course it wouldn't. It would be just like buying a sheep: the seller would claim that his animal was a world champion and the buyer would say it was fit only for the knacker's yard. Somewhere in between was the truth – and a price both would be happy with. Yiannis was emphatic that if the parties couldn't agree neither side should take offence. This was important to us because if we couldn't get the mule's stable we still had a lingering interest in the olive mill and thus might yet become residents of Afrata. We didn't want to get on the wrong side of anyone in the village.

Kyriacos was a direct man, once he got started. He came to the point quickly and stated his price. We made our counter-offer. Our negotiation cha-cha had very few steps in it – just five, in fact – but what we agreed must remain a secret. Kyriacos became our very good friend and, in Cretan village society, financial dealings between friends are definitely a private matter. Suffice it to say that he was happy and so were we!

Unfortunately, Kyriacos rather expected our negotiations to conclude with me handing over the money straight from my pocket, Cretan-style, from a grubby wad of notes. In return he would have signed a note saying that the land was ours. Obviously he hadn't been involved in any land dealings for a long time. Things had moved on and now all property sales had to be registered and have tax paid on them. Yiannis confirmed that the deal had to be done properly with a formal contract drawn up by a lawyer, even in Crete! Kyriacos knew that Yiannis's daughter-in-law, Marianna, was a lawyer in Hania. Would she help? Yiannis telephoned her at home. We could all go and see her in the morning.

The sun was sinking behind Afrata's back wall of mountain but we decided to take another look at "our" site before driving back to Hania. It was very quiet. Eastwards, the White Mountains were pink; everything seemed bathed in warm light except for the darkening wall of mountain behind us. It was a good place to be. We drove back towards Hania and decided to stop on the way for a celebratory dinner. The bill for dining out is pretty much the same wherever you go in western Crete and, in any case, a heavy bill wouldn't guarantee good food and service. Right on the main road we saw a taverna named after an insect – the Tzitzikas – and, tickled by the name, decided to stop there. It was a good choice. When we complimented the cook-proprietress on her home-cooked rabbit *stifado* (a casserole) and her red wine she sat down with us and chatted for a while. She became the first person with whom we shared our news of the purchase of the piece of land in Afrata. "That's wonderful – Afrata is my family's village!" she said, shaking our hands and wishing us happiness there. We described Kyriacos's plot, which she identified immediately. "Very beautiful," she said. "What views! The sea, the mountains…You'll like it up there!" She asked our names and introduced herself as Katina Tzitzikaki (literally, "Katina the little cicada"). We left a generous tip with the bill, but before we got to the door Katina stopped us and handed it back: "You paid too much," she said, with a friendly smile.

We wanted the purchase of the land tied up quickly, with the contract signed and sealed before our return to England, which was now just a couple of days away. In Marianna's office we learned to our dismay that there wasn't time for a proper contract to be drawn up because we needed a *topographico* – a surveyor's plan – of the site and the little building on it. She offered a solution: a preliminary contract in which Kyriacos agreed to sell and we agreed to buy, subject to everything being as we had been told. We would pay over the money and Kyriacos would promise to give it back if we were dissatisfied with anything. We felt well disposed towards Kyriacos and so we agreed. Marianna knew a reliable surveyor – called a civil engineer in Greece – who would draw up the plan for us. Would we like her to ring him? We felt that we could trust her as well and we were happy to let her make the arrangements on our behalf. We asked what her fee would be: it was a fraction of our last solicitor's bill for house-buying in England – and the service was definitely more personal and distinctly less stuffy.

The preliminary contract was drawn up and it was agreed that the surveyor would make the plan within a few days. Kyriacos, like many older Cretans, had no bank account and, after paying over a small deposit there and then, we promised that as soon as we were back home we would arrange for the remainder of the money to be transferred to the main branch of the National Bank of Greece in Hania. Kyriacos would have to collect it in person, in cash. That was it. We had two more days in Crete, where we now almost-definitely owned property – a stable with magnificent views! It was obvious that we would have to return to Crete again quite soon. We weren't sorry. The only blot on the horizon was our unsold house back in England.

CHAPTER SIX

We resolved not to visit Afrata again before we went home. There was nothing more we could do there so we decided to become tourists and take a holiday from both house-buying and thinking about house-selling. Anyway, we had a hobbyhorse to ride. We were heavily into roadside shrine-spotting and it was an activity that guaranteed to enliven any journey in Greece.

The first shrine I ever saw was a crude little box structure at the edge of the main road into Athens from the airport. It was my first visit to Greece and I was thrilled by the sight of this totally "foreign" object. The taxi-driver reluctantly agreed to stop while I took a closer look. It was little more than a metal box with its door and two sides made from glass. It was about the size of a hatbox and stood a metre or so off the ground, on a braced tripod of angle-iron. It was finished in white and topped off with a slightly crooked cross. Above the door, runny red paint had been used to inscribe a crude dedication to Agia Paraskevi (St Friday), a Greek Orthodox favourite. Inside was a cheap, printed icon of the saint – showing her with a cross in one hand and a dish of eyes in the other – and an incense burner and a small wick floating in a glass of olive oil. The smoke from the burning wick and from the smouldering, tarry incense escaped through a gap above the door and Paraskevi's soot-streaked name suggested that she might have been martyred at the stake. The taxi's harsh klaxon sounded a sharp reminder of the here and now and I got back in the car. The taxi-driver said over his shoulder, "You'll see plenty of those. They put them up after road accidents, you know." As we drove along I checked them off; after a dozen or so in half-a-dozen minutes I stopped counting. It seemed that the roads of Athens were lethal.

That first encounter was the start of a long and continuing interest in the shrines, which had caught my attention because of their primitive "artistic" qualities rather than their religious function.

Susan was already familiar with the shrines, of course, but she admitted that she had accepted the commonly-held view that they were just the sad little reminders of tragic road accidents. There were so many of them around that only the most unusual ones ever caught her attention. Together we started to take photographs and collect whatever information we could, with the intention of producing an illustrated book, *The Wayside Shrines of Greece*. We discovered that a road accident was just one of many reasons for the construction of a shrine and that there was no such thing as a standard design or a list of "approved" construction materials.

Unfortunately for our book plan, we had struck on a genuine minority interest. It seemed that we were the only two shrine-spotters in the world! Many allegedly educated Greeks take the view that the shrines belong to "low" culture and are therefore unworthy of serious attention. The rest just don't care. We tried to interest a Greek cultural organisation in our project and were brought face-to-face with the dismissive contempt that "sophisticated" Hellenes have for the shrines. We tried to present our view that they were an important aspect of Greek popular culture; a genuine folkloric art form, constructed for reasons which were inseparable from the Greek Orthodox faith that moved their makers. We even proposed a direct link with ancient Greece, where simple columns topped with the head of the god Hermes could be found at the front doors of houses and along the roads. Our listener, a power-dressed executive Hellene, was not going to have her prejudices disturbed. "These shrines are just peasant rubbish!" she dismissively told us.

After that, we concluded that perhaps people would have to be taught to develop sensitivity to something as idiosyncratic as a wayside shrine. It's true that they are not "Fine Art", but they are sincere, direct and individual. They are true to their purpose and even though they abide by the conventions of the faith that inspires them they rarely become merely conventional. They may at times be crudely built but they are never coarse. You do not have to be Greek Orthodox – and you most certainly do not have to be a peasant! – to be amazed by them and to rejoice that there are still individuals in an increasingly materialist world who want to express their feelings by making something for others to see. For us, the shrines come alive at night-time, and I made that the start of my introduction to our yet-to-be-seen book:

The twilight flickering of olive-oil lamps in wayside shrines makes a pilgrimage of every journey along the roads of Greece.

No traveller can fail to see the shrines. They serve as sentinels at the edges of all Greek roads. The bright light of day exposes their vulnerability to assault by careless traffic, to the ravages of time and to the scourge of pollution, but as night falls the mantle of darkness transforms them into magic lanterns, beckoning to passers-by.

The shrines are legion. They stand in their infinite variety as the idiosyncratic expressions of the belief of individuals in something beyond themselves; they are the way-marks of unknowable routes that all of us must follow.

The shrines, with their complements of iconic saints, are also works of art. Most are the constructions of ordinary people, innocently engaged in creating a genuine folk art. Greek shrine-builders work intuitively within the traditions of an open-minded society, and while the ideas of others may be borrowed there are no rules to follow or to break. The only guiding influences come from an individual creative impulse and the desire to glorify.

Shrine-spotting's in our blood now, and book or no book we go on taking pictures and talking to people. We left Hania and drove westwards, looking forward to finding a few more little gems to add to our bulging slide archive. We were now very selective and found only a few reasons to stop before we reached the outskirts of the village of Episkopi, not far to the south of Kolymbari. We wanted to see the unusual circular Byzantine church dedicated to the archangel St Michael and noted for its frescoes and mosaics. The Rotonda, as it is better known, was in the charge of a jolly young monk called Melkhizedek, which was also the name of the last bishop to have had his see there. Marauding Turks had slaughtered Melkhizedek I – along with his flock – on the spot.

We looked around the church, noting a fine fresco of St Michael and a very early depiction in mosaic of the Christ-sign of the fish. Outside were the excavated graves of the ancient monastery and a delightful walled garden in full bloom. The setting, away from the road and amid trees and fields, was tranquillity itself.

We chatted to Melkhizedek II about the building and the archaeological excavation work, which remained in progress although currently dormant. He was very well informed. At one point he even produced two plastic carrier bags full of human bones to reinforce his account of the church's sad history. This action had a melancholic effect upon him; he sighed deeply and put the bags down. We were the only visitors and our host smiled his way out of his apparent sadness to ask us if we'd like to sit in the garden and have coffee with him. Melkhizedek made three Greek coffees in his open-air kitchen and then we all sat around an old electrical cable-drum that made a perfect garden table. The ancient church was on one side of us and tiers of geraniums on the other.

Before he had become a monk, when he was still called Sophocles, he had opened up the church to visitors. Now, established in the state of monk-hood and renamed Melkhizedek, he wanted to re-establish the monastery that had previously existed there. He was a very relaxed and apparently happy young man, although given to sighing and looking into the distance. However, it was never long before he returned his attention to his listeners, bestowing one of his winning smiles as he did so. His twinkling eyes suggested that he enjoyed a good joke. His presence at the Rotonda was due to some mystical experience involving St Michael, the details of which remained a little vague to us. We sipped our coffees and then Melkhizedek turned his attention directly on me and asked: "What does St Michael mean to you?" It was exactly the sort of penetratingly sincere question that I wasn't equipped to answer to his satisfaction just like that. The plain truth was that St Michael didn't mean a thing to me, but I couldn't tell him that. If only he had asked me, "What is the sound of one hand clapping?" I might more easily have waffled out an answer, but "What does St Michael mean to you?" floored me. In my desperation, the Marks & Spencer brand name flashed into my mind. It was the product of a kind of word association. Unfortunately, the next word to come along was "underpants". I could hardly tell him that what St Michael meant to me was a pair of underpants! Susan looked across at me and encouragingly said, "You were baptised...?" Of course I was! I looked straight into Melkhizedek's face and declared, with relief: "Well, I was baptised in the church of St Michael and All Angels, at Lancing, in the south of England." He beamed, leaned forward and patted my shoulder, exclaiming: "That's wonderful!" Then, eyes definitely twinkling, he said, "You know, most of the English who come here tell me about underpants..." I gave a hollow little laugh while he chuckled away. Some other visitors arrived and so we thanked Melkhizedek for his hospitality and got up to leave. He walked with us back through the church and we stopped in the doorway to make our farewells. "Goodbye, my friends," he said, "and by the way, St Michael was a Jewish angel. That's probably why Mr Marks and Mr Spencer chose him!"

Ten minutes drive away we came across a shrine at the site of a road accident. A car, long-since abandoned, had obviously collided with the shrine and now the two were as one, tangled together and embowered with greenery. It was a rare scene epitomising the popular view of the purpose of shrines. The mystery is that such sights are so rare, given the appalling standard of Cretan driving. Take signalling, for example. The most-favoured signalling technique of the Cretan driver is to flick on his hazard-flashers. This has a range of possible meanings, none of which will be clear to the observer until after a manoeuvre has been executed. It could mean that the driver intends to turn left *or* right or that he is planning to reverse into you. You'll only know at the last second. The use of the hazard-flashers suggests that the electrics are in working order on most cars. Not so! Although all cars now have two brake lights, most Cretan drivers seem to think that one is more than enough. Indeed, it's not that uncommon to see – that is, if you're lucky enough to see it before the collision – a car with no lights at all. These are just the visible (or not!) defects; it doesn't do to dwell on the general state of such hidden essentials as brakes and steering. Greek traffic law says that cars must be roadworthy – and there's a compulsory MoT-type test to see that they are. While this law applies throughout the whole of Greece, in western Crete it is not enforced at all. This is because there is no official testing centre. The nearest one is in Iraklion, about 100 kilometres from Hania, and no Cretan is going to drive that far in a car that might be unsafe!

The roads are not lawless, however. The police set up roadblocks from time to time and pick on likely-looking cars for a spot check of insurance certificates or the wearing of seatbelts, which Cretans seem to think is unnecessary if you have an icon dangling in your windscreen. Unfortunately, the police are hampered in their work by drivers who have gone past unchallenged. Perhaps out of gratitude for having got through the roadblock unscathed, they vigorously flash their headlights to signal a warning to oncoming drivers. The alerted drivers immediately slow down and adopt the respectable demeanour of totally law-abiding citizens – or look for a detour so that they can by-pass this challenge to their freedom to drive dangerously at speed, without lights or insurance.

Road rage doesn't seem to be a problem but tailgating is so common a practice that it looks as if it might be a required part of the Greek driving test. Cars zoom up behind you, so close that you can no longer see their headlights, and stay there, matching your speed, kilometre after kilometre. They either wait for the road ahead to swing into a blind double-z bend, in which case they suddenly overtake you, or they just disappear from your rear-view mirror by turning off down a side street. Although Cretans are supposed to drive on the right, the most-favoured position is slap bang in the middle of the road. The situation's not much better when they're no longer in motion. The middle of the road, sharp bends and the corners of awkward road junctions are all favourite parking spots. In Hania, when the traffic police aren't around, people seem to park wherever they like, obstructively, dangerously and with a total disregard for other road-users. An odd local custom rather encourages them in this anti-social behaviour; before writing out a parking ticket, the traffic policeman will blow a loud whistle two or three times to warn the offending driver that he should shift his car. The illegal parking thus goes unpunished and will be repeated one minute later just around – or on – the next corner. Of course, if the driver doesn't come running then the ticket gets written.

Slow-moving agricultural vehicles, especially the aged three-wheelers that look like petrol-driven lawnmowers and which splutter along, fouling the air, are a hazard wherever you meet them. Cyclists tend to prefer the inadequate pavements, so they are generally a danger only to pedestrians. The users of other two-wheelers – mopeds, scooters and motorbikes – are usually a hazard only to themselves. The law is quite clear: crash helmets must be worn. It may be that the law neglected to say that they should be worn on the head and that could explain why it's so common to see a motorcyclist speeding along with a crash helmet dangling from his elbow. A sidecar is a rare sight in Crete but a family of four on a two-seater scooter isn't. Cretans, who love children and cosset and indulge them, are strangely ready to perch their offspring on an overloaded two-wheeler and risk life and limb lurching along on road surfaces that are at best uneven and, yet more often, potholed and broken.

The daftest road-users of all, though, are definitely tourists. They come from northern European countries where they are obliged to obey well-enforced traffic laws and where road safety is a major concern, officially and personally. Once in Crete, and with an ignition key in their hands, they go bonkers. Young and not-so-young couples hire scooters or "easy-rider" motorbikes, which they can barely control, and cruise around without helmets or any other protective covering save for a pair of swimming trunks or a bikini. They seem to think that the roads are absolutely safe and that the sun shines only on the beach. Deceived by the cooling effect of the air when riding along, they expose themselves to the hot sun until they look like lobsters, their sunburnt shoulders and legs promising a night of agony. For such as these, optimistic plans for a holiday of sun, sea and sex soon give way to shade, nausea and calamine lotion.

A hire car may look safer than a scooter, but the way some tourists drive it's a wonder they ever make it to the end of their 14-night package. Cretans are generally dreadful drivers – and a lot of Cretans would agree with that – but they tend to be relatively relaxed when behind the wheel. That may explain a lot of their poor driving technique: they are inattentive drivers, more interested in chatting or smoking than in concentrating on the road ahead. Tourists who hire cars are either so tense and nervous that they crawl along, never getting out of third gear, or otherwise they spray themselves with pheromones and go in for aggressive and threatening displays of top-doggery. Either way, they're a menace. They provoke the otherwise-tolerant Cretans and encourage the worst excesses of their already-bad driving habits. The best advice for any road-user in Crete is to drive defensively – and invest in an icon! Sobered by such considerations we drove off in search of lunch and another shrine or two.

It's a popular misconception that religious observation – at least in its practical aspects – is more the domain of women rather than men. We never found this to be true of the Greek Orthodox church, where although "ladies first" is the rule, men are seldom far behind. Take the shrines, for example... We stopped to explore another village, in which we encountered a shrine as tall as a man but twice as broad and built from old hand-made red bricks, which were about half the size of modern English bricks and had an appealing soft, weathered look about them. Although the shrine was substantial and gave the impression of having been built to last, the incongruous blue-and-orange, floral-patterned curtain stretched across its doorway on a piece of string suggested something more temporary. We found the original wooden door, now rotten, propped up against the side of the shrine. We drew back the curtain to reveal a cavernous interior housing a host of icons, including one of St Minas, who was decapitated in 296 AD because he had refused to renounce his Christian faith. As recently as 1941, Minas had been credited with preventing two German bombs from exploding on a church named after him. This followed his triumph of 1826, when he appeared on horseback, apparently with his head on his shoulders, and single-handedly dispersed a horde of marauding Turks bent on destroying the same church. Now his memory was celebrated here. He was an unusual choice for a shrine-builder and we looked around for someone to talk to. Coming up the road was an old lady, dressed in black. She was a typical Cretan *yiayia* (grandmother). Susan greeted her and asked if she knew anything about the shrine. "Like what?" she snapped. "Well, why was it built?" prompted Susan. "I don't know!" barked the old lady. "My father-in-law built it, you'd have to ask him." I made a conservative calculation that her father-in-law would have to be at least 95, but it was possible he was still around; Cretans live long lives, barring accidents. "Could we talk to him?" asked Susan. "He's not here. He's on holiday in Australia," she declared. He had obviously acquired some of the fortitude of St Minas! We said we might call by again sometime. "Suit yourselves," she said.

The village had a taverna offering a very simple traditional dish called *fava*, which is a yellow lentil puree served with olive oil, raw onion and olives. It is a staple of the much-lauded "Cretan diet" which holds out the promise of a long and healthy life for its followers. The shrine-builder holidaying "down under" probably owed his active old age to the consumption of food such as this. *Fava* is a very basic pulse dish and, with the addition of a fresh green salad, the village baker's crusty bread and a glass of red wine from the barrel, tasty enough for you to want to clear your plate. It isn't special in any way; it's just plain, good food to leave you feeling that you've eaten well. We sat in the taverna garden, with a dessert of slices of chilled watermelon, and discussed our plans. Tomorrow would be our last complete day in Crete. We decided, after all, that we would revisit Afrata.

CHAPTER SEVEN

Breakfast over, we walked the few minutes to the wide esplanade in front of what locals often – and quite properly – refer to as "the old Firka", an Ottoman fortress on the seafront, alongside which we always parked our car. Nearby could be seen one of Hania's occasional lapses into the ridiculous: the bright red toy-town "train" – a string of carriages drawn by a make-believe engine on pneumatic tyres – that wended its way slowly around the streets, clanging a bell and tugging a cargo of self-conscious tourists. Few of the passengers on this absurd vehicle ever looked really comfortable. The children were usually frowning, while the adults sported the fixed half-grins of people caught in a supposedly enjoyable situation from which they wanted only to escape. Another oddity on offer was a "champagne tour" in a gondola. At this hour, the covered boat could be seen bobbing vigorously in the harbour, not unlike a champagne-cork on a storm-tossed pond! As far as we knew, there were no canals, Venetian or otherwise, in Hania… We were glad of the dull anonymity of our hired Fiat Panda.

We took the new national road from Hania to Platanias. This is a stretch of virtual motorway but without central crash barriers, a proper hard shoulder or emergency telephones. However, it had so many trees and shrubs planted along its edges that one day it would be like driving through a park. The road is part of a plan to link the east and west of the island with a major highway and newly-constructed bits are suddenly revealed here and there along the proposed route. One day it will be possible to drive from Hania to Kolymbari without touching the old coastal road. We had, of course, already experienced the new – and already collapsing – stretch in operation between Kolymbari and Kastelli.

We approached the now familiar but no less awful crossroads at Kolymbari and turned right following the sign for the monastery. The mountain road up to Afrata had been a daunting challenge the first time we took it, but now it seemed tamer. The sea was still down there, to the driver's right, but an instant plunge into eternity now looked merely possible rather than probable. Passing the signpost for the Evelpidon monument, a war memorial on a headland high above, we saw that someone had dumped two old lavatory pans, a sink, some rubble and a broken rabbit-hutch on a patch of flat cliff-top which had clear views across the sea to the distant Akrotiri peninsula. It was the sort of place where in England people would park and enjoy a picnic. We stopped to have a really good tut-tut about it and to our horror discovered that there was rubbish everywhere, over the cliff, along the rocky shore and back up the valley that ran alongside the steep road to the memorial. On the other hand, one man's poison can be another's meat… Back home we never left a builder's skip unrummaged and we prided ourselves on knowing good rubbish when we saw it. We felt our displeasure modify slightly as we made our first Cretan finds: a pair of very solid decorative iron gates, slightly bent, an old curlicued metal garden seat, also in need of repair, and a battered, semi-circular, painted metal water-can with a tiny brass tap – exactly airline cabin-luggage sized! We would have taken them all straight up to Afrata but for the limitations of the Fiat, which unfortunately could take only the can. Susan remembered having a can just like it 30 years earlier. It had hung on the wall over the sink in her kitchen in Boyiati, then outside Athens but now one of the sprawling city's suburbs. In those days Boyiati did not have mains water and such a can, which held about five litres drawn from a well, provided the supply for washing and drinking.

At the entrance to Afrata we encountered a one-eyed shepherd fixing a sign to a post above the oil drum-kennel of one of the two chained dogs. Our curiosity led us to stop the car and get out. He told us that he'd had to ask someone to make the sign for him because the dogs had been let off their chains. He suspected passing tourists who probably thought that they were striking a blow for animal rights. The sign was in German and English. It read: "PLEASE do not unchain the dogs – they've the task to keep the goats from entering the village. Thank you." Were the dogs being treated cruelly? Their situation certainly looked unenviable when compared with that of an English pet dog but then life is very much harder for the average Cretan hound, most of whom seem to be expected to do something to earn their keep. These two definitely weren't indulged in any way but they had food, water, shelter, an occasional walk and they weren't going to be shot at as sheep-worrying strays. The odd thing was that even after being released the dogs' strong sense of duty kept them at their posts and they would hang around their bins waiting to be re-chained! Nevertheless, they presented an unhappy picture; so much so that when we got back to England, "You'll end up as bin dogs!" became another of the empty threats we waved at our two pugs whenever they misbehaved themselves. The most remarkable thing about the bin-dogs was that anyone ever got near enough to unchain them without doing themselves an injury by skidding on a dog turd. The ground around the bins was a no-go area and the sign could have just said: "Keep out! Minefield!"

The next sign along the road was the one marking the start of the village. It was in Greek and English, but the modern, demotic Greek word for Afrata confusingly appeared with an extra accent just before the initial A. This extra initial accent is totally unknown in modern Greek – and it's not an ancient Greek "breathing mark" either. It showed that the road sign had obviously been made when the government was still using a now-defunct form of Greek known as *katharevoussa*. This was a high-falutin' variant invented by and for the newly-independent state's ruling elite in the 19th century. The right-wing colonel's junta of 1967-74 was the last regime to actively promote its use. One day, the sign would become a collector's item, along with similar ones still to be found standing outside quiet villages.

We drove straight into a dilemma in Afrata. The owners of the Kali Kardia and the Asteri *kafenea* were both keeping an eye out for passing trade. They spotted us simultaneously and we got a hearty welcoming shout from one and a friendly wave from the other. We couldn't go to both so we decided to go to neither. Instead, we returned their greetings and went up the steps into the community office, a sort of two-roomed "town hall" and doctor's surgery, on the pretext of wanting to read the public notices posted there. My eye was immediately caught by a beautifully-calligraphed and decorated certificate, unfortunately more than slightly foxed and moth-eaten, despite its frame. It was a post-war testimonial from the New Zealand Government, signed by the then prime minister and by General B. C. Freyberg, VC, the British-born leader of New Zealand's forces during the Second World War. It was addressed to the people of Afrata, gratefully acknowledging the sacrifices and risks that they took to help the many "kiwi" troops who avoided capture by the Germans in April 1941 and either joined the partisans or made their escape to Egypt to rejoin the fight as regular soldiers. This relic was the sole exhibit of interest to us. We skimmed the notices – which all seemed to be about sheep or olive trees – and then we set off on foot to explore the village further.

Visitors approaching from Kolymbari pass the cemetery and the church and then find themselves at a crossroads, flanked by the unexciting village square and overlooked by the two *kafenea*. We knew that a left turn would soon take us on to the open road to Astratigos and that straight ahead was the uphill route to our site. We took the unfamiliar lower road, to the right, serenaded by the screeching of hordes of invisible cicadas, and discovered that Afrata had another half. So far, we had only seen Upper Afrata, but there was also a Lower Afrata. The road wound downhill, past another, much larger, *kafeneon* whose interior had been fitted out like a cocktail bar – although the barman had abandoned the expected white shirt and bow-tie in favour of a singlet vest. He had an excuse: in this weather, cocktail shaking would probably work up quite a sweat! Then there was a children's playground – obviously now well into its middle age – that had been erected by "The Cultural Society of Afrata". Olive groves flourished on both sides of the road. We passed the remains of an elderly and unknown pale blue three-wheeler car called an Alta, although some of the now-exposed components bore the winged H of the Heinkel logo. There was a shrine, yet two more *kafenea*, and houses old and new. On the right, a sign appeared: "BEA H". We followed this road, which continued to wind downhill. Houses soon gave way to a lane, hedged-in by lush greenery, which would not have been out of place in Devon. We entered a gorge, at the start of which a church had been built into a cave high above the road. With each step, the gorge became wilder, an impression furthered by the large birds of prey wheeling in the narrowing strip of sky above our heads. Huge, fissured cliff walls began to cloak us in; only the three witches and their bubbling cauldron were missing. Then the sea came into view and the dramatic gave way to the delightful. The narrow road down through the gorge had brought us to a little bay, pebbly but clean and undoubtedly a good place for swimming. We sat for a while. It was very quiet, just the lapping of the waves and the distant bleating of some sheep to be heard. Two fishing boats passed by the mouth of the cove but the beach remained ours.

We arrived back at the square in need of refreshment. It hadn't been a long walk back, but it had been uphill all the way – and it was hot. We climbed the steps to the shady terrace of the Kali Kardia. The proprietor formally introduced himself. Kostis knew that we were buying the plot of land up above; Kyriacos, the seller, was his brother-in-law. He treated us to two bottles of lemonade and after a good-humoured interrogation, in which he succeeded in finding out, among other things, our names, how old we were, what we did, where we lived in England and how many children we had, he wished us good luck with our purchase. Walking away from the *kafeneon* I told Susan that I had forgotten to tell Kostis my inside-leg measurement. "Why would you tell him that?" she asked. "Well, he knows everything else!" I said.

The steep road leading from the square up to the top of the village was just wide enough for a single car, but it was a short road which existed only to serve the houses built along it. At its end, it became the footpath that we used to get to our site. Just before the old olive mill, a lane branched off to the left. It was a cul-de-sac with one attractive old stone house, embellished with a vine and masses of geraniums, another that was brand new, and some that were rather nondescript and which it would be impossible to date. From one of these a woman emerged and greeted us. Susan introduced us as the people who had bought Kyriacos's plot. "I've heard about you," she said. We were now just behind the Kali Kardia, and I wondered if Kostis had already beaten the drums of

Afrata's bush telegraph. Her husband appeared and they introduced themselves: Stavros and Eleni. He was a fisherman with a boat in Hania and they only came out to the village to pick their olives or for a break from life in the city. The big new house belonged to Stavros's brother, who was a builder in Athens, and it was used only for family holidays. The old house belonged to some "foreigners" who appeared just once or twice a year. It seemed that in the summer the Greek population of Afrata was swollen with refugees from the sweltering heat of mainland Greece. Eleni invited us in to eat. They were going to have fried eggs and we were welcome to join them. Over our eggs, which swam in olive oil, and some bread and wine, we talked about life in Afrata. Stavros, a son of the village, assured us that it was a very friendly place. In fact, he didn't have an unkind word to say about anyone.

We left our new acquaintances and continued on up the hill, passing a house dated 1888. Another road led off to the right; it was also a cul-de-sac, this one containing a couple of goat sheds and more old houses. We retraced our steps and continued on towards the house of Yiannis and Dimitra, which was really distinguished not so much by its lemon tree as by a huge purple Bougainvillaea arched over the gateway. Yiannis had probably

told us to look out for his lemon tree because in his mind it was a much more important thing than a mere woody shrub, however striking. There was no one around so we carried on along the footpath only to be stopped in our tracks by a woman dressed all in black and with a scarf tied eccentrically around her head in a style that looked very Bloomsbury-ish. She was sharp-featured and rather bird-like, tiny and frail-looking but alert and cheerful. She was, however, very old; her pale skin was lined and wisps of fine white hair strayed out from her wrap-around headgear. Our presence obviously puzzled her; she didn't see many strangers on this path, which ran past her well-kept front yard. We introduced ourselves, again as the buyers of Kyriacos's plot. There was nothing wrong with her hearing! She was delighted and shook our hands and wished us every joy. We told her our names, and this caused another flurry of delight. Her name was Antonia Kalitsaki. She said to me, "We have the same name day!" Greeks don't bother too much with actual birthdays; instead they celebrate the "name day", that is the day dedicated to the orthodox saint whose name they bear. So St Anthony's day, the 17th January, is when everyone called Anthony ("Antonis" in Greece) or Antonia gets wished the equivalent of "happy birthday". For un-orthodox names, like Tarquin or Candida, Darren or Cindy, then there's the moveable feast of the omnibus All Saints' day, which falls eight weeks after the Greek Easter Sunday. Old Antonia insisted that we let her cook something for us and nothing that we could say would dissuade her. She was a poor woman but she did keep chickens. Would we like eggs? What could we say? We watched as she cooked them in a battered old frying pan over a wood fire in her yard. Ten minutes later we were sitting inside, in her cavernous living room, eating the morning's second helping of fried eggs, which we were beginning to think might be Afrata's staple food. Very good eggs they were, too, but we would have preferred to have had them another time.

Back outside, Susan complimented Antonia on the gnarled vine, heavy with grapes, which spread from one corner and provided a green canopy over the whole yard. Antonia looked at it nostalgically and told us that she remembered it being planted when she was a child. After promising her that we would visit often when we lived in Afrata, we went on up to our site. It was just as appealing as the first time we saw it. We climbed up on to the roof of the old stable and clearly saw the start of the gorge that we had walked before our two lunches. We didn't stay long. On the way down, we saw that Yiannis and Dimitra had reappeared. They invited us into their house and when we told them that we were returning to England the following day Dimitra looked quite concerned. She pulled open her refrigerator door and produced a bowl of eggs. Susan and I looked at each other. She caught sight of our anxious glances. "What is it? Don't you like eggs?" she queried. "No, it's only that we've just had four – each," I said. "These are for you to take back to England," she explained. Our sighs of relief were audible. The village ladies think it unlucky to place an egg directly into someone's hand, and as most women still wear aprons this doesn't usually present a problem: the eggs are gathered in one's lap and the apron becomes an impromptu bag in which they can be safely carried back home. We didn't have aprons so Dimitra muttered something that might have been an incantation and put our eggs in a box. We thought we'd be lucky to get them home unscrambled. While she was doing this we told Yiannis that we had seen the framed certificate thanking the people of Afrata for the help that they had given to New Zealand soldiers during the war. "Not everyone in Crete helped them," he said darkly. He began to tell us about collaborationists but Dimitra, having finished with the eggs, interrupted him to ask us if we had any plastic containers. "Not on us," I confessed. She bustled off into her scullery and returned with some of her own. Despite our protestations, she gave us a large bottle of her own olive oil and three litres of wine from the barrel. Unexpectedly loaded with these welcome gifts, we made our farewells. They wished us a safe journey and said they hoped we would make a speedy return. I wanted to come back, even if only to hear more from Yiannis about Cretan quislings.

Driving away from Kolymbari, Susan spotted a bright blue metal shrine just off the road. It had an olive tree on one side, a fig tree on the other and a donkey tethered nearby. The scene was almost biblical. It was a small shrine and had four very bent legs stuck into an irregularly shaped lump of concrete. We stopped for a better look. It was dedicated to St George and apart from the crooked legs, it was well-made and in good order. The donkey idly surveyed us and then brayed loudly. The noise brought an old man from somewhere behind the fig tree. He reluctantly conceded that it was his shrine, as if he went along with those people who said that it shouldn't be of interest to anyone else. Susan explained that we were making a collection of photographs of interesting shrines and he was obviously encouraged enough to tell us his story. He had had a dream in which St George had commanded him to build a church. The dream was obviously very powerful because when he woke the old man remembered it clearly, but unfortunately, the memory of it also brought deep feelings of despair because he didn't have the money to pay for the construction of a church. That's when he had the idea of building the shrine. It would be his little church! He got a local metalworker to make it for him and then he set it proudly at the edge of the road on four sturdy legs. It stood for less than a day before a passing tractor knocked it over, buckling the legs. When the old man tried righting it, it could no longer stand up straight. That's how it came to be in its present position, set back from the road, and firmly re-anchored in a lump of concrete.

We had noticed earlier that in Nea Hora, a sea-front area west of Hania's old harbour, there were a number of interesting-looking fish tavernas and we decided that we would have our dinner in one of them. We knew that it would be our last dinner in Crete, this trip, but we were trying hard not to acknowledge that fact by remaining "in denial" about tomorrow's inevitable three hours of airborne purgatory – the charter flight back to England. Our standard rule-of-thumb for choosing a taverna was applied and so we sat down in the one that looked as if it was the choice of Greeks. It turned out to be very Greek. I ordered swordfish and Susan went for the sole. My fish arrived and I waited for Susan's to come. She urged me to eat. I started, slowly, but it was so delicious that I couldn't just nibble at it. I had almost finished before the waiter could be asked about the whereabouts of the sole. "It's on its way," he said cheerfully, without even the slightest hint of an apology. My plate was clean when the sole arrived. As Susan had watched me eat, now I watched her. After she had finished, I signalled to the head waiter, who was standing surveying the diners. I asked him why the swordfish had been served before the sole was ready. The question was obviously unexpected but it got his full, albeit rather pained, attention. "Well, sir, most of our Greek customers generally share their dishes. That's why the swordfish came first and was put in the centre of the table and you were each given a plate. Then, afterwards, you could have shared the sole when that arrived," he explained. I asked him what we should do if each us actually wanted only what we had ordered. "Just tell us," he said. Ah, well...

We strolled back along the sea front. In the darkness, Susan suddenly chuckled. "What is it?" I asked. "I was just thinking about that last flight home from Athens," she said. I remembered it. Our seats offered a grandstand view of the lavatories and a young woman with a toddler had just bolted herself into one of the cubicles when the pilot warned that there was turbulence ahead. A steward bounded down the gangway and began pounding on the cubicle door. It remained firmly shut. "Come out!" he yelled while hammering on the door. Nothing. The pilot's voice came over the air: "Well, the turbulence doesn't seem to be as bad as we thought..." The steward pressed his face close up against the lavatory door and shouted: "You've got 30 seconds and then we're coming in!" He reached for a master key and just as he yanked the door open, the pilot announced, "Nothing to worry about, ladies and gentlemen, we're now in the clear. You can leave your seats if you want to." The young woman's voice could be heard to shout, "How dare you!" She then leaned out of the cubicle and yanked the door shut again. The red-faced steward stalked off to the rear of the plane and a few minutes later the woman with her toddler came out, looking as if absolutely nothing had happened.

CHAPTER EIGHT

We were back in Kent; in a cottage that was indisputably still ours. There were no letters or telephone messages to tell us of queues of would-be buyers urgently wanting appointments-to-view or of generous offers made sight-unseen. There were, however, two calls from double-glazing firms offering to fit the very latest aluminium doors and window frames... I wanted to telephone the estate agent but first we decided to collect our two dogs, Pug and Mavros, from their holiday hideaway, the local kennels at Green Man Farm, so named because of the pub next door. At least, the pub had been called The Green Man two weeks earlier, when we had deposited the pugs with Mr Simm, the proprietor of the kennels, but things move faster in Kent than in Crete. Now the pub was a born-again roadhouse modishly re-named The Frog and Orange. We approached the kennels, curious to see if Mr Simm had followed suit and called out the sign-writers. He hadn't. As we walked with him from his house towards the kennels, he looked up at the cloudy Kentish summer sky, with its promise of rain, and said he liked the idea of Crete. When we suggested he took a holiday there, he shook his head like a man burdened: "I'd love to, but who'd look after all these animals?"

We could see our two dogs stretched out in a pen, like two sausages on a plate. Pugs are funny little dogs. They're myopic, can smell a rat from as far away as six inches – but no further – and are very selective listeners. They have only one expression on their wrinkled faces, and that's moral indignation. They have no bite and their bark is worse than silly. Their short, curled tails sit on their backs like furry meringues and move imperceptibly, unlike the vigorous windscreen-wiper tail-wagging of most canines. There was no doubt, however, that the fawn Pug and his adopted brother, the black Mavros, were overjoyed to hear our voices. In the pen, they gave us a smothering welcome, rubbing their squat, squarish bodies against us and nuzzling us with their snub noses. Then they raced around in circles – in their case, this was the tail wagging the dog – and after a final lap of honour they celebrated the family's return to normal life by simultaneously urinating on a gate post. After that, they sat on our feet, as if to stop us abandoning them again, while we settled up with their host.

Back home, we were unpacking our suitcases. Susan yelped and pointed into hers: a scorpion nestled in the middle of a T-shirt. It was a Cretan scorpion, small and capable of inflicting a powerful sting, but not lethal. Nevertheless, he was an unwelcome souvenir. I got a tumbler and a piece of cardboard and carefully trapped him. "Now what are you going to do?" asked Susan. I told her that I was going to release him outside. I think I might have been a Buddhist in a previous existence because I found it impossible to kill insects, with the exception of fleas, flies, mosquitoes, sheep ticks, wasps and woodworm. I carried the little scorpion downstairs and out into the road, where I set him down, but instead of scuttling away he just stood there. A speeding lorry swung around the nearby bend and I stepped back into our driveway to avoid being flattened. The sluggish scorpion was not so lucky. His crushed body could be seen embedded in the asphalt. The lorry had been carrying pesticides. It was probably karmic retribution.

There now seemed to be an unbridgeable gulf between the mule's stone-and-rubble stable and the thatched cottage. When I rang for an update, the agent was blunt: "No interest whatsoever. Sorry!" We thought about changing agents but when the proposed new one suggested, in impeccable agent-speak, that we could "achieve a rapid sale" if we offered the house at less than we'd originally paid, we left our faith where it was and continued to wait for something to turn up.

Gypsy Court was the problem which overshadowed all others. Ownership meant that we were tied to the treadmill of high outgoings. We could manage, but the price was the suspension of all our hopes for a different kind of life and while we waited for things to happen Susan became the main breadwinner. My contribution to the domestic budget had become a mere crust –

but, of course, it would be worth more than that if we ever got to Crete. Once upon a time I had earned two salaries – one from college lecturing and another from *The Sunday Times* – but I had lost both, although not simultaneously, which made their loss a misfortune rather than carelessness! If I had wanted to I could have held on to the college job, teaching university graduates the elements of print journalism, but I wanted to leave and the opportunity offered by the pension could not be ignored. It had been somewhat different at *The Sunday Times*, where, on Fridays and Saturdays and during college vacations, I had been the newspaper's editorial odd-job man. I enjoyed my work and liked my colleagues, but while I beavered away re-writing readers' letters for publication or contacted our man in Val d'Isere for a report on skiing conditions, the newspaper's managing editor, like blind Pew in *Treasure Island*, prepared to press into my hand the black spot signalling redundancy. The generous pay-off and the prospect of rediscovering the weekend discouraged me from challenging his decision, although it was obvious that all my jobs would still have to be done by someone. I didn't realise it at the time, but letting go of that work was the first step on my journey to Crete. The same managing editor had earlier failed to entice me to give up teaching and join the newspaper's foreign desk full-time, taking on the job that Ian Fleming, James Bond's creator, had once done. At that time, the college was a very cushy billet and I was reluctant to relinquish it. Had I done so I would have been 65 before any kind of pension came my way.

My limited income obviously wasn't the fast lane to a new life in the sun but that was only because of the torpid housing market. If we couldn't sell the house, our Cretan adventure would have to be put on the back burner. The longer we waited, the more irksome Susan's work became, not least because of the tortuous daily commuting from the sprouting fields of east Kent to an office at Hyde Park Corner, and although I was making art I was certainly not making it pay. Apart from a nebulous sense of personal satisfaction, the returns from my labours varied between nugatory and negative but were mostly just plain non-existent. As I looked at my monthly pension "pay-slips" I began to feel that I might yet become grateful for any writing job – even one filling out parking tickets. We could both feel the prospect of a new life in Crete slipping away into an indefinite future.

We still had to send Kyriacos the outstanding balance for the purchase of his plot. I instructed the bank to make the arrangements. The clerk was fazed by the idea of sending a large-ish sum of money to a man who didn't have a bank account; she wanted to refer the matter to a senior manager. I told her that it was my money and that I was happy with the arrangement. She seemed genuinely concerned that I would simply be despatching my money into the ether. However, after much humming and hawing she relented. Afterwards, I decided that her doubts about the transaction had had nothing whatsoever to do with concern for me; she was acting just like those humourless and self-important building-society clerks who attempt to police British personal finance by suspiciously eyeing every transaction. I'm sure the bank clerk, just like her building-society colleagues, suspected that my transaction was linked to the laundering of ill-gotten funds from drug dealing! Her insistent attitude – "but you *must* have his bank account number..." – reminded me of when, after a road accident, I was taken to one of the few remaining fully-functioning hospital casualty departments. Although I was riven with pain and barely conscious, my initial treatment consisted of being badgered by a clipboard-tapping administrator who wouldn't accept that I couldn't remember my postcode! It won't be long before every British citizen is registered at Swansea and given a number-plate to wear, back and front. One day, at the hour of our death, an electronic voice will boom out of the sky: "Come in Number E257TKP. Your time is up..."! The relentless onward march of northern Europe's computer-assisted bureaucracy is another reason for moving to Greece, where in many places they've only just got the hang of carbon paper and a well-chewed ballpoint. Anyway, five days later Kyriacos walked into the main Hania branch of the National Bank of Greece, where, unlike their British counterparts, the clerks didn't automatically suspect his probity; he established his identity and collected the money. The finalisation of the deal had moved on a stage but it was about to take a small step backwards...

Back in Hania, Marianna, our lawyer, had warned that before the contract could be finalised and the land registered in our names we might have to get statements from the tax authorities, showing that we did not owe the state any tax. Susan told her that the Inland Revenue seemed to have a piece of paper for every eventuality... Marianna chuckled. "Not your tax office in England! The one here, in Hania." Now she telephoned to say that foreigners were not exempt from the tax clearance requirement. "But we don't pay any tax in Greece," Susan told her. That wasn't the point, as Marianna was quick to point out. Tax dodging is the Greek national sport and the authorities had hit on an idea for putting the squeeze on reluctant payers. Houses, land, second-hand cars – even mobile 'phones – all of these were now impossible to obtain without the production of an official tax clearance certificate. For us, as foreigners with UK tax records, getting the clearance was a formality but we had to apply for it in person. Although this was unwelcome news, we weren't in any hurry. Gypsy Court wasn't going anywhere and we felt confident that we could delay our return to Crete until September, when the weather would be a little milder. We would then also start discussions with our civil engineer and his architect-partner about designing a house and apply for a building permit.

The English summer was passing away and already there was a hint of autumn in the air. I had always found the arrival of autumn a depressing time and, for me, it was justification enough for moving to Crete. Earlier, though, our spirits had risen. The estate agent had telephoned to say that two people had asked for details of the house and now wanted to view it. Two! Although it was still summer, as far as the housing market went, it turned out to be a false spring. The agent's details clearly stated that the house had six acres of land, but the first viewer, a woman on her own, was obviously spatially challenged. "Is that six acres?" she asked, staring suspiciously from one of our upper windows. "Definitely!" I countered. "It's rather...big," she hesitantly offered. "What did you think six acres would look like?" Susan asked. We watched her as she ran her eye over our lumpy, rectangular field and made a mental calculation. "About one acre," she answered. She was followed by a sniffy couple who liked the cottage but were obviously put off by the total lack of rustic charm in its surroundings. As we stood outside the front door of the cottage, two hot-air balloons drifted overhead, the flames from their burners clearly visible directly above our thatched roof. The balloonists waved down at us; they had misread the situation if they thought we were glad to see them. I knew that our viewers would use this totally unexpected apparition as the excuse to disentangle themselves from us; after all, fire is the one thing all thatched-roof owners live in constant fear of. "Well, thank you," said the woman. "It's a very nice cottage but I'm afraid those balloons would be a problem. You see, we wouldn't want to be overlooked..."

A few weeks later we took the pugs back to Mr Simm and went on to Gatwick for the plane to Crete. It was a charter flight whose complement of passengers included a group of ebullient northerners who entertained themselves by singing "Viva Espana!" – with a gusto that increased after every can of lager. Had they boarded the wrong plane or did they think that Hania was on the Costa del Sol? Either way, their behaviour made a tedious journey excruciating and when the aircraft landed we were the first out of our seats for a quick getaway. Our repeat hiring of a Fiat Panda, arranged from England, was generously upgraded to a canary yellow Renault Twingo and so we drove off towards Kolymbari in a degree more comfort and conspicuousness than expected. We thought next time we'd book the Twingo in the hope that we might be rewarded with a four-wheel-drive Toyota Land Cruiser. Everything seemed so familiar – particularly the appalling behaviour of other road-users. We were hungry; we had eaten only the cream crackers from the in-flight meal. The Taverna Tzitzikas appeared ahead of us on the left and that's where we stopped. Katina Tzitzikaki greeted us as if we were old friends; she even remembered our names – well, half of them! In Greece, Susan is invariably called Susannah, and that's what Katina said, but Antonis somehow became "Alex", and I didn't have the heart to correct her. We accepted her recommendation of chicken with okra, with which she served a welcoming gift of a jug of red wine from the barrel. This was only our second visit! I contrasted it with Broadstairs, the Kentish seaside town where I had visited the same almost-empty pub with the same companion every Wednesday night for a dozen years, always drinking three pints of the same draught bitter. In all those years, the pub never recognised me as any kind of "regular". It was yet another reason for coming to live in Crete.

We had booked into a hotel in Kolymbari so that we could be on Afrata's doorstep. We drove up to the village in the evening and were loudly greeted by Kostis, who was on the lookout, as usual, from the terrace of his *kafeneon*. He poured us two *tschikoudias* – on the house – and asked us about our plans. We didn't have too many at that point so it was a short conversation. We were joined by Kyriacos, who lived just across the road. He gave us another warm welcome and ordered Kostis to pour us two more *tschikoudias*. Kyriacos had an invitation for us: he would like us to come to his house the following evening to meet his wife. "We'll drink some wine together," he said. "What time?" I asked him. "Come early," he said, and the settled look on his face showed that that was all the answer I was going to get. It was definitely never like this in Broadstairs!

The next morning, it was a Wednesday, we went to Marianna's office in the centre of Hania. She was going to take us to the tax office – the *ephoria* – and hold our hands while we took our first steps into the unknown waters of Greek bureaucracy. They turned out to be murky. It was nine when we arrived at our first port-of-call within the unprepossessing and grimy tax office building: the untidy ground-floor room where they would issue us with a slip of paper confirming that we were up-to-date with the payment of our water bills. There was no computer in evidence, just a massive ledger, but this remained unopened and my own say-so seemed to be authority enough for the clerk to hand over the required slip of paper. It was a painless experience but without our guide we wouldn't have known about this simple first step – or the whereabouts of the water-bill office. The tax office was definitely not user-friendly: there were no helpful leaflets, there was no central information desk and, except on the staff-only lavatory doors, no proper signs. On each floor there were a lot of identical glass-fronted offices, most with little arched windows for the public to stoop down and shout through, but few of them clearly displayed what it was that they did behind the glass. It was quite common for people to stand in line and then be told that they had come to the wrong room. In a few cases, compassionate clerks had stuck up handwritten notices to help people through the labyrinth of the tax system. There were queues everywhere and at the head of each one there would be a knot of people all jostling for the clerk's attention. The jabbering noise made concentration difficult and thick clouds of cigarette smoke had the same effect on breathing. It was also very hot and stuffy; the only ventilation came from people fanning themselves with sheaves of tax-papers.

On an upper floor, the three of us joined a queue leading to a little window above which was stuck a grubby DIY notice from which it was just possible to infer that tax-clearance might be the matter handled here. Fortunately, it was. Marianna got me to sign a prepared statutory declaration to the effect that I'd never been liable for tax in Greece, which she then handed to the clerk, together with the water-clearance slip. The clerk put them to one side. "He still needs a personal tax reference number," she smiled and pointed behind us to another queue in front of another little window. Here the pushing and shoving was of Greek national standard, but our lawyer's experienced elbows got us into pole position and another slip of paper was duly handed over. We returned to the back of the tax-clearance queue. Marianna, like lots of the Cretans here, killed time chatting with various friends and acquaintances who just happened to be passing by. Such is life in Greece that everyone ends up in the tax office at some point! The tax-clearance certificate, complete with a number, was handed over and Marianna led us off to another office where we would register the details of our purchase.

Now we were going to have to pay some tax on the purchase of the land. Three factors govern the amount of this tax: the size of the plot, the price paid and its whereabouts. For every town and village there is a regularly reassessed table of values, which is influenced by what people say when they come into this office. It's no good claiming to have paid only 500,000 drachmas for a piece of land that the official table shows to be worth 2,000,000 drachmas. Even if you did pay only 500,000 drachmas they'll still tax you on 2,000,000! On the other hand, if the official table shows a value of 2,000,000 but you paid 2,500,000, then you can confidently understate what you paid. Here, northern Europeans, who may well have paid too much, are a problem for their new Cretan neighbours. Their frequent filling-in of official forms threatening the direst of penalties for telling anything but the truth, the whole truth and nothing but, has frightened the sense out of them. They're so scared of getting into trouble with the authorities that even when they don't have to, they state to the last drachma what they paid for a house or piece of land. This has two consequences: first, they pay more tax than they really need to – and the percentage rate is high; secondly, the higher price, now revealed to the authorities, leads to a reassessment of the table of values and local Cretans are forced to pay tax on land values far higher than the real – and sensible – market price. The tax authorities make no allowance for daft foreigners paying silly prices for plots of land; they just allow the inflation of local land values to occur because it means more in tax revenues. We were well within the norm for Afrata so for us there was no point in fibbing! The clerk calculated how much tax was due and wrote us out yet another slip of paper which we had to take to another office for ratification by rubber-stamp before he could make out the actual bill. Marianna waited with us to see that the amount of tax was approved and then she left us, saying, "I'm sorry. I've got work to do." We understood. We ended our visit standing in our longest queue yet – the one for the cashier. Despite the large amounts of money involved, all payments had to be made in cash. We got to the head of the queue and received the official receipt that would allow us to proceed towards the drawing up of a proper contract and the subsequent registration of the land in my name. I looked at my watch. It was still Wednesday, but three hours had elapsed. I began to think that there might just be an argument for centralised computer systems.

We returned to Marianna's office via the civil engineer's, where we picked up our *topographico* – the site plan – and made an appointment to meet with him and his architect-partner. We handed Marianna the tax receipt and the *topographico* and she told us that she would pass these to the notary public, the *simvoliographos*, with whom she had already arranged a meeting and who was the only person authorised to prepare the final contract. We were to return to Hania the following morning, bringing Kyriacos with us.

In Afrata that evening, Kyriacos raised no objection to the trip to Hania and we agreed to drive up from Kolymbari at eight o'clock in the morning to collect him. Now we discovered that an invitation to drink wine meant an invitation to eat. Cretans drink wine only at mealtimes; *tschikoudia* is a different matter – they'll drink that at any time between getting up and going to bed, although they'll often nibble something with it. We had arrived at the Platsakis family home to find the dinner table set for 12 people. We felt embarrassed; we had obviously come at an awkward time. Kyriacos introduced us to his wife, Petrula, who welcomed us and then ushered us into seats at the table. This dinner was for us! Dishes began to appear from the kitchen – and people from various doorways. We recognised Aristides, Kyriacos's son, who introduced his wife, Irini, and their two teenage sons, Kyriacos and Yiannis. Male names are quite straightforwardly confusing in Greek society: the first-born son nearly always takes his paternal grandfather's name so, in the extended families that are still typical of Cretan villages, you'll always get more than one response if you shout out a name. Greeks have an obsession with lineage but for quite different reasons from the petty snobberies of English genealogy. Parents' names are part of one's identity and form-filling in Greece always requires that you give them, making you sound like someone from the pages of mythology. I became known as "Anthony, Son of Albert and of Doris…" There were a lot of names as people continued to appear, but one thing was clear: they were all related. Some stayed to eat and others just popped in. Although we were the objects of their attention, Petrula's food deserved – and got – the most interest. There was a lot of it. There was a *pilafi*, the heavily-buttered rice dish which Petrula served with a mound of boiled chicken – from which two monstrous claws protruded! There was a deliciously rich rabbit *stifado* and two plates of little roasted birds, suspiciously thrush-like, which had apparently been hunted down by the Platsakis boys. We passed on these. Plates of chips, *mizithra* cheese, *horta* and mixed salad completed the spread, which was noisily and heartily consumed with knives, forks and fingers. The wine was superb. It was old – and strong. With every glass, Aristides toasted me: "Antoni! *Bomba!*" You didn't need a word of Greek to know that this stuff was explosive. It was a thoroughly enjoyable dinner party, Cretan village style, in which we had been the main topic of conversation. Our hosts couldn't understand why anyone would want to leave England to live in Crete. We tried our best to explain, but they seemed unconvinced. They could not grasp the essentially semi-detached nature of English life; they could easily understand passionate involvement but not disengagement. To them, the concept of alienation sounded like something cooked up by a German sociologist!

CHAPTER NINE

Kyriacos was waiting for us, along with two other villagers who wanted a lift down to Kolymbari. Afrata had just one bus a day, and most adults avoided it if they could: it was the school bus. By all accounts, travelling on it was the same sort of nightmare that it would have been in England. I can remember when English schoolteachers still took some responsibility for their pupils' public behaviour. In those days, they would do "bus-stop duty" and try to protect expectant mothers, old-age pensioners and other innocents from the scrum of delinquent juveniles who, given half the chance, would trample anyone who got in the way of their scramble upstairs for a soothing post-school cigarette. Of course, the bus that collected the children from Afrata and other villages was not a double-decker but...

Parking is not a problem in Hania, provided that you're prepared to walk a little. Poor old Kyriacos was having trouble with his legs and had developed a distinctive rolling gait that led some unkind villagers to say, "Here comes the boat!" Nevertheless, he stoically refused to allow us to drop him near the *simvoliographos's* office and insisted, despite his obvious discomfort, in walking in his rolling way through the narrow back streets of Hania with us. We arrived at the office and endured more than two hours of tedium as the contract was brought step-by-slow-step to its finalisation. The *simvoliographos* was a pleasant and efficient woman, and her office cool, calm and well-appointed, but it was still irksome to sit there while her secretary carefully word-processed the contract into existence and then for the three of us to have to listen while page after page was read out aloud to ensure that we all understood what we were letting ourselves in for. This particular legal requirement was undoubtedly a survival from the days of illiteracy. We were eventually liberated by the flourish of a pen and the plastering of the document with lots of gaily-coloured official tax stamps, most of them illustrated with reminders of the ambiguous truth that justice is blind. Then, like most Cretan professionals, the *simvoliographos* asked for her fee in cash.

We returned to Kolymbari and dropped Kyriacos at Aristide's metal-bashing workshop, where fences, gates and suchlike were made to order. We then went on to the local land registry and lodged our contract. As of now, we were the indisputable owners of land in Crete. After lunch, we drove southwards from Kolymbari for a short excursion. Beyond the villages of Spilia and Drakona, we came across a battered sign in English: "The Ancient Church of Holy Stephen. Builded...A.D." Unfortunately, time, the elements and someone with a shotgun had erased the date when it was "builded". There seemed to be only one-and-a-half parking spaces for visitors, and they were on a sharp bend in the road. We parked as carefully as we could and walked along a narrow country lane, flanked on either side by tall, deciduous trees. It was shady, green – and damp. Grass and bracken grew profusely and the stone walls along the lane were moss-covered. It was very un-Cretan. Ahead of us appeared a crooked but charming little chapel with sloping white walls and an undulating red-tiled roof. It sat under a huge canopy formed by trees which had grown up on either side. The setting would have been idyllic but for the lines of untidily draped electric cables just above head height and the scores of discarded plastic cups and screwed-up tissues scattered all around. The chapel's tiny interior consisted of a single room, about 12 feet long and eight feet wide, frescoed from floor to apex with biblical scenes. The interior had obviously been restored at some time because the frescoes formed a patchwork with irregular shapes of rough pink plaster. It was gloomy inside. There were only two small windows and although a naked bulb hung down from the ceiling – from a hook that had been crudely hammered in above the head of a saint mourning the death of the Virgin Mary – there was no switch that we could see. We left the door wide open and got just enough light to enjoy this apparently Byzantine gem, although there was not a scrap of information anywhere to help us understand where we were or what we were looking at. Although the floor was level, the interior walls seemed to tilt, like a ship rolling to starboard. On the left of the recessed altar there was a fine portrait of St Stephen himself. In fact, most of the faces looked as if they had been drawn from life and in their mediaeval costumes the characters had a Chaucerian quality. This place deserved more attention than it was obviously getting. By the entrance there was a particularly engaging fresco of some malignant-looking soldiers laying hands on St Stephen, but it was sickening to see that someone had hammered a bright plastic-and-metal electrical staple into this. We sat outside for a while, on some incongruous new park benches, ignoring the litter and the cabling, and enjoying the tranquillity of the place and the coolness of its green, woodland-like setting. No one else came and after 20 minutes or so we returned to the car, dismayed by the all-too-common Greek disregard for ambience.

On our way out of Kolymbari, we had noticed a sign to Marathokefala and the Cave of St John the Hermit, a local saint who had originally moved from Egypt to Cyprus and then, presumably, to this cave. At least, that's what we assumed because once again there was no information to help the curious visitor. The asphalted road to the cave had climbed until we found ourselves high up above Kolymbari with splendid views of the sea and of olive groves stretching away for miles. We were the only visitors. The cave was in a hilly area dense with conifers – and its surroundings were a lot tidier than those of the lovely little chapel we had just left. Someone here had taken upon himself the Herculean task of trying to control Greek litterbugs. On a eucalyptus tree, much carved with initials, there was a sign urging people to be tidy. In capital letters it admonished: "CLEANLINESS=CIVILISATION!" Unfortunately, the sign's postscript – "Don't wound the trees" – was obviously ignored by the many people who came armed with pocketknives. Visitors arrived first at a little chapel, which was no more than a walled-in cave, with its electricity meter cunningly hidden behind a hinged icon of the saint. Beyond was a much larger – and open – cave, lofty and almost cathedral-like, set out for religious services with "rustic" timber seating for about 500 worshippers and standing-room for many times that number. There was a permanent, and rather worn, nativity scene and positioned rather oddly above it some old farm implements, including an iron plough and a wooden yoke. A short flight of steps led down to a tiny cave referred to as "the crypt of the saint". All in all, the whole place was dank, like most caves, but the blue sky was always visible through the entrance and the surroundings, aromatic with pine, invited visitors to linger. It would be a very pleasant place for a picnic.

In the evening, we drove up to Afrata to say hello to Yiannis and Dimitra. We sat and drank *tschikoudia* in their sitting room, which like most such rooms in Cretan houses was decorated with numerous framed photographs of family members. Greeks are also very fond of certificates. Yiannis had one, with an accompanying medal, testifying to his part in the war – which for Greece ran from 1941-45. The certificate, however, was dated 1987. People of Yiannis's political colour, which was indisputably the deepest red, had to wait that long to have their contribution officially recognised, such were the ideological problems of life in post-war Greece. The Platsakis sitting room was similarly decorated, but there the certificate told of the involvement of Georgis, the elder son of Kyriacos and Petrula, in the Greek military adventure in Cyprus in 1974. Yiannis invited us to return on Sunday, telling us to come early in the morning because it was a special day. The twinkle in his eye suggested something unusual and we readily accepted – while hoping that whatever it was it didn't include boiled fatty mutton. Dimitra asked Susan if she would buy something from the supermarket in Kolymbari and bring it up to Afrata on Sunday. It was a cleaning spray and she gave Susan an empty container so that there would be no mistake.

Back at our hotel, Susan, desperately looking around for something to read, picked up Dimitra's empty container and took it into the bathroom. Seconds later there was a loud burst of laughter. "Listen to this," she called through the *en suite* door. "This label is a classic: *'The new special liquid extra PLAY POL makes the of thread absorbents parquetezes and the dustclothes magnetics.*
'Release you from the tiring floor washing, while the dusting at home at office or shop, does a really game. His special qualificative synthesis, refresh, keep up and give back the lost

shining in: Durable parquete, plastic floors, marbles, tiles, furnitures e.t.c.

'APPLICATION INSTRUCTIONS: Spray well and same the parqueteze or the dustcloth and clean. The result will be inflaming you!

'Note: If you have not bottle with vapourize you can sprinkle with the insertion.

'Extra PLAY POL circulate as a spare part also. Singly placing the valv of vapourizer from the first bottle'. That was all *sic!*" she exclaimed and repeated, "*'The result will be inflaming you!'*"

The following morning we set off to drive beyond Kastelli to explore the westernmost road that led through Platanos to Sfinari and beyond. After Platanos, the mountain road became spectacular and exhilarating. It was a very high and exposed road of varying widths and variable condition. One misjudged moment of impetuosity could be the last; it was a very long way down to what would definitely be an unhappy landing. The views were breathtaking and encompassed sea, sky and mountainside, but mostly sea and sky. The only blot was the acres of plastic-sheet green-housing looking like so many Monopoly buildings on the flat plains along the edge of the sea, way down below. There wasn't much traffic, which was a relief, but like the road to Afrata there was the hazard of colliding with a wandering sheep or goat around each bend. Warning signs consisted mainly of the traditional Greek impromptu kind. The authorities seemed to install crash barriers on the basis of a bit here, a bit there – but often none where you might reasonably expect to see some. Local villagers had supplemented this protection with their own. Every now and again a length of string would be stretched along the edge of the road. This string was slender protection but it was a clear warning to proceed with extreme caution; it represented a little local knowledge of dangerous things. The road was also frequently way-marked by pyramids of carefully balanced stones, which showed the spots where the edges were subsiding – nearly always on the seaward side. It was an exciting road to travel, but I wouldn't want to do it in the dark. For a rally-driver it would be a dream route, chock-full of thrills, but we were in someone else's sedate little Twingo!

The road turned inland at Sfinari, which sported too many "rooms to let" signs for it to be an unspoilt place, so we determined to drive on for a while longer. A few kilometres up the road we came to a signpost for Melissia, which seemed to be high up on a mountainside. I turned and we found ourselves on a road that discouraged progress. The poor old Twingo dipped and lurched from rut to rut and over stretches of broken concrete. Turning around didn't look any easier than carrying on, so we carried on – into country that was steadily getting wilder and wilder. The road snaked upwards between massive chestnut trees; the temperature was discernibly cooler. Was there a village up here? There was little sign that anyone made much use of this road. Around yet another bend we came across a donkey tethered at the foot of a gully. Further on we saw our first signs of human life: a small cemetery. Beyond this some ruined stone buildings gave way to a little church and a dusty area that would pass as the village square. This was Melissia. It was very quiet. As we stepped out of the car, a voice from above said, *"Yassas."* We looked around and up and saw that we had been greeted by one of the villagers, who was leaning over her fence. *"Yassas.* Is there a *kafeneon* in the village?" I asked. "This is the *kafeneon*," she said and gestured for us to come up. It didn't look much like a *kafeneon*; it was more like someone's yard, with its basketball hoop, pot plants, cat and obviously long-unridden vintage BMW motorbike. A bottle of Cretan lemonade is more refreshing than most fizzy drinks and we drank two while the *kafeneon*-keeper asked us where we were from. When we told her about our plan to live in Afrata, she threw up her hands. "Ah! I know people from Afrata – Yiannis Dagounakis is my cousin." Although Greeks call Crete "the big island", it is obviously a small world! When we told her that we already knew Yiannis and Dimitra, she introduced herself as Kostoula and told us that Yiannis had been born in Melissia but had moved away in the 1920s. There were still many members of the Dagounakis clan in and around Melissia, however. We chatted about the village; it was little more than a hamlet and definitely way off the beaten track. Kostoula said that tourists were rare birds up here. Our offer to pay for the drinks was waved to one side but we were enjoined to take her regards to Yiannis and Dimitra.

Melissia was carved out of the mountainside and the roads, of which there were few, went whichever way they could. There were big trees all around, through which magnificent distant views opened up. It was a very cool and leafy place. We came across some spectacular ruins, including two old olive mills, with their huge manual presses sprawled on the ground, but saw only two or three people – one of them a very cheerful old lady with a Zimmer frame accompanied by three playful kittens! The ride down the mountain track required as much care as the ride up, but Melissia had been worth the effort.

The drive back was marginally less terrifying because we were now on the landward side of the road. As we reached the outskirts of Kastelli, we decided to stop at the first taverna to come into view. We were gamblers when it came to eating out! That's how we ended up parked outside The Stork, a large double-fronted place in need of a lick of paint and with a redundant supermarket and a scrubby bit of wasteland as its neighbours. It was unappealingly situated right on the main highway, opposite a boat-chandler's, but redeemed somewhat by a screen of flowering shrubs along the edge of the road. The taverna's peeling noticeboard advertised "traditional Cretan dishes". The Stork was a perfect example of the problem of deciding where to eat; Greece is a country where appearances are deceptive. The gleaming new exterior of a modish restaurant may hide a cook with well-honed culinary skills while the authentic-looking taverna may be using live traditional music to mask the sound of its overworked microwaves. The Stork looked unprepossessing but behind its sad and dusty facade there was a talented cook, a varied menu of fresh fish, meat and vegetables, exceptionally good wine and prices pitched at the pockets of working Cretans.

The broken entrance door slid open, not very easily, to reveal what could have passed for an English "caff" of the sausage-egg-and-chips variety. It was obviously a good "caff". The customers were Cretan workmen and where there were still uncleared tables, all the plates had been wiped clean by satisfied diners. Between two huge glass tanks of goldfish, a step led down to a larger dining room furnished in a somewhat plusher style, with mirrors, a wallpaper-mural of a municipal park such as one might see in a Yorkshire town, and, perched on a long wooden bar, a well-stuffed stork whose outstretched wings sheltered a redundant espresso machine. On the wall behind this masterpiece of taxidermy was the bearded head of a *kri-kri*, the original long-horned wild goat of Crete. We debated where to sit. There was no one in the "restaurant", so we joined the patrons of the "caff", choosing a table by a wall on to which had been pasted another mural – an enormous, badly-printed and wholly irrelevant picture of a lake in the Canadian Rockies.

The proprietor approached with a paper tablecloth, like a bullfighter carrying a cape. The tablecloth was allowed to float down and settle itself; two menus were handed to us. Most Greek eating-places serving ready-cooked meals, such as *pastitsio* (macaroni casserole) or *moussaka* (aubergine and ground lamb with white sauce), display them in a glass-fronted cabinet so that customers can see what's on offer. The Stork had such a cabinet but the glass was so heavily steamed-up that the contents remained a mystery. Susan asked about the day's "specials" and was answered with a volley of Cretan vernacular from which it was just possible to catch what was on offer. We ordered a plate of little fishes, beef *stifado*, *soudzoukakia* (savoury rissoles), with *horta* and potatoes. I asked if there was "loose wine", the local red wine from the barrel. The proprietor looked at me like a man deeply shocked by an unexpected insult and, stroking his very Cretan moustache, said, "Certainly!" He stepped away from the table and then turned, raised an eyebrow and asked in a puzzled way: "You like Cretan wine?" "Certainly!" I said. He smiled and nodded.

The proprietor didn't seem to be the sort of man who could fawn upon customers or gush false *bonhomie*, even if his life depended on it. His style was close to what Greeks call *"poly varys"*; he displayed a *gravitas* that masked a natural good humour. In truth, he was a committed *restaurateur* who cared about the food he served, which was also the food he ate. Without doubt, his food was the best that we had eaten anywhere in Greece – and the wine, his own, had all the character of its maker. It was intended to be taken seriously, but not soberly – and there was nothing impulsively perky or chirpy about it! Imbibed slowly, it encouraged warm, deep, mellow thoughts and discouraged wasteful physical exertion. When he came to the table with our modest bill, I told him that we had found the food and the wine first-rate. It was a compliment he seemed to expect and he acknowledged it with a slight nod at a nod. "Would you like some more wine?" he asked. Yes, but not now! If we hadn't been driving we would definitely have accepted his offer. We chatted a little and he expressed, in suitably sombre tones, how disappointing he found the occasional tourists who came into The Stork. "Omelettes and salads, omelettes and salads," he sighed. Then, with a visible shudder, he added, "…and mineral water!" It pained him to see tourists turning up their noses at prime fresh cuts of locally-produced meat simply because they didn't look anything like the supermarket's offerings back home. "They want everything lean and off-the-bone. Flavour doesn't matter to them – only the appearance!" he exclaimed. Fresh fish is an unbeatable dish in Crete, but he couldn't understand why tourists seldom ate it – nor why they drank bottled wine rather than his own. I couldn't explain these mysteries of the tourist trade either, so I settled for telling him the truth: the loss was all theirs. He greeted my remark with a slight upward nod, a raising of one of his extraordinarily mobile eyebrows and a barely-perceptible twitch of his curling moustache, all of which combined to suggest a sorrowful resignation. With only the slightest movements, he appeared able to express an enormous range of feelings. We asked him to give our compliments to his chef. "My wife, Epistimi," he explained. When we asked him his name, he made a dignified bow that came from another age and replied, "Dimitris Anagnostakis." After that first visit, The Stork became *"to steki mas"* – our regular eating-place.

When looking for somewhere to eat, a crowded taverna doesn't necessarily mean a good taverna, unless most of the customers are Greek. Of course, not all Greeks know bad food when they see it, but a place packed out solely with northern European palefaces may well owe its popularity simply to "recommendations" from tour guides or holiday "reps" who get a kickback from tavernas for this kind of head-hunting. One taverna proprietor told us he paid out 500 drachmas for every punter who came in this way. The Tzitzikas taverna, at Kamisiana, had taken a long time to establish its summertime trade because of its refusal to pay such kickbacks, but it had become a very popular place with tourists – and Greeks – simply because of the efforts of the hard-working Tzitzikakis family. The blandishments of restaurant touts should generally be ignored, as should their frequent behind-your-back insults when you refuse their invitations. On the other hand, not every taverna with a tout is bad. Where there are a lot of eating-places, the competition for custom is intense and a tout becomes an evil necessity. Similarly, not all places that open only for the summer take a grab-the-money-and-run attitude to their customers. The first taverna we visited in Hania, the Karnagio, offered first-class service and food, but stayed firmly shut during the winter months. It is very difficult! The best one can say is that there are things to be suspicious of, such as those visual menus consisting of colour photographs that deteriorate so rapidly that they look like illustrations of bacteria cultures in petri dishes. Menus themselves are not much of a guide anyway; most places offer pretty much the same sort of fare, although too many items on a menu could mean a heavy reliance on the freezer and the microwave. The more tarted-up a taverna, the less likely it is to be authentic, and in this case one should definitely look askance at places which leave the olive oil in a little jug on the table rather than present it to you on your food. This practice is intended solely to satisfy those tourists who haven't yet got the message that olive oil is good for you.

There is one copper-bottomed rule: avoid any place where all the chairs have seats woven from thin rope – unless you're a masochist or believe in acu-pressure! Rush makes a comfortable seat, but hard, shiny and knotty rope first corrugates your backside and then numbs it. You'll spend the entire mealtime squirming around and flexing your buttocks. The only good thing is that concentrating on your behind will provide a distraction from indifferent food, but if the service is also slow your suffering will become interminable. Of course, one could always go armed with an inflatable rubber-ring, like a haemorrhoid-sufferer, but that would rather take the shine off dining-out... If you think there's a better seat somewhere else in a taverna, then go for it! No Greek taverna-proprietor worthy of the name will ever tell you where to sit and if you want to rearrange his furniture to suit yourself he won't object to that either. It's nothing like the situation in those British restaurants – usually Indian or Chinese – where the waiter adamantly insists that you sit at the worst table he can offer, even when you're his only customer. I've not stayed to eat in many such places.

That evening we had a meeting with Dimitris, our civil engineer, and Nikos, the architect, a busy man whose portfolio of responsibilities apparently included rubbish collection in Hania. Whatever else happened, we'd probably end up with our dustbin in the right place! I had already roughed-out some ideas for the "living machine" that we wanted built and these were not dismissed as the wild ramblings of an amateur, as they would have been by more professionally precious northern European practitioners. Dimitris and Nikos were obviously into air-conditioning and picture windows but we soon got those removed from the agenda. The peculiar problems of our small site – which was only about 200 square meters – were discussed and Nikos undertook to rough out some ideas for us to consider on Monday.

CHAPTER TEN

It was Saturday. Tomorrow we would be going to see the Dagounakis but today we were off to the Platsakis. Kyriacos had invited us during one of the many dull moments in the *simvoliographos's* office, raising an imaginary glass as he did so. We arrived in Afrata at mid-morning to the now-usual shouted welcome from the two competing *kafenea*-keepers, Kostis and Stephania. We parked our car on the *plateia*, in the shade of a tamarisk tree, and walked the short distance to Kyriacos's house, which seemed very crowded.

Kyriacos introduced us simply as Antonis and Susannah to people we had not met on our visit a few days earlier. There was Kyriacos's other son, Georgis, and his wife, Tula, and their two sets of twins: Kyriacoula and Petrula were 19 years old and Georgis and Dimitris were just five years old! Kyriacoula and Petrula were with their husbands and their own offspring, daughters born within days of each other. Petrula's husband, Nektarios, was big; he looked like a trencherman; Stavros, Kyriacoula's husband, was a little smaller. Georgis, the paterfamilias of this branch of the Platsakis clan, shook hands, looked at me rather lugubriously and asked: "Do you wear rubber boots, Antoni?" I wondered if this was a euphemism, but if it was I couldn't think what for. Kyriacos stepped in and with a big grin began to mime marching-on-the-spot: "Squelch! Squelch!" he said. At that moment, Aristides' Toyota truck arrived, heavily laden with grapes. The mist cleared. Today was the day the Platsakis family would tread their grapes for next year's wine and we had been invited along to help. Some grape-treaders wear rubber-boots to help squeeze out more juice and to protect themselves from various nasties hidden in the bunches underfoot. Others think that rubber-boots are rather sissy and, more importantly, you lose the sensual delights of the warm and sticky must from the newly-crushed grapes oozing between your toes and up around your ankles and the scratchy-tickly feeling of the stalks underfoot. The Platsakis family were bare-footers to a man.

The Toyota's luscious load was shovelled into a stone-built treading-trough – a *patateri* – belonging to the Platsakis's patriarchal-looking neighbour, Stratis, one of Afrata's elders who could often still be seen riding around the village on his donkey, with his wife following on behind, on foot. The *patateri* was about 10 feet square, with a rendered floor that sloped gently towards a runaway that emerged on the outside as a stone spout from which the liquid must from the trodden grapes could easily be collected. It was a traditional design and such constructions could still be seen outside many old houses. In Melissia I had noticed one that had an ancient piece of carved olive wood as its spout. Other variations included steps to make access easier and little niches for the safe-keeping of "refreshments". Aristides satisfied the requirements of hygiene by sprinkling our feet with water. Then he shouted, "Ready!" and – just like an up-and-at-'em paratrooper yelling, "Geronimo!" – vaulted over the waist-high wall and squelched straight into the mountain of grapes. Georgis finished his cigarette and eased himself in, like a man entering a swimming pool. Nektarios and Stavros rolled themselves over the edge of the wall and splurged into the grapes, which visibly rose in the *patateri*; I wanted to shout, "Eureka!" I was the last man in, entering this new experience gingerly. There were now five of us in the *patateri*, although sandwiched as I was between the two big fellas it seemed like more. Petrula appeared and gave each of us a sprig of aromatic basil to wear behind our ears. No wine-treader is considered properly dressed without this traditional garland. Kyriacos stationed himself by the spout to oversee the rough filtering of the must and its transfer into the wooden barrels in his cellar.

The treading began, slowly at first and more-or-less on-the-spot. Gradually it developed into an odd little dance of half-a-dozen steps forward and then the same number backwards, varied with an occasional circular stomp. Aristides left the *patateri* to help Kyriacos, and Georgis took charge of the treading. In the kitchen, Petrula and her two daughters-in-law, Tula and Irini, were busy boiling some of the must to reduce it to a sweet dark-brown treacly substance called *petimezi*. Every now and again Georgis ordered a halt to shovel down more fresh grapes from the mound that had been built up in one corner. Sometimes the must flowed too quickly and we had to sweep the juice back with our feet while he blocked the drain-hole with a bunch of dried thorns. There didn't seem to be a wastage rate in this operation. The treading became more energetically dance-like and attracted spectators who leaned on the wall and nibbled at the lumps of grilled liver and drank the *tschikoudia* that Petrula had provided for the workers. The merry-making Aristides poured all the treaders glasses of *tsichkoudia* and handed me one with a shout of, "Antoni! Cretan whisky! *Bomba!*" The stomping got livelier and Nektarios and Stavros larked about with their own lewd version of a conga. This Dionysian scene now had a new audience: a passing middle-aged Scandinavian couple had braked to witness this unexpected glimpse of village life. They got out of their lime-green hire car and Aristides welcomed them with *tsichkoudia*, which they accepted tentatively. They ignored his advice on how to drink it – down the hatch in one go to a shout of "white bottoms!" – and sipped it slowly, like linctus for sore throats. When he gestured that they should get in the *patateri*, they fled!

Kyriacos suddenly appeared at the *patateri* wall carrying something covered with a cloth. A halt was ordered. It looked as if a religious rite was about to be performed. The cloth came off the mysterious object, which turned out to be an ancient hydrometer. Silence reigned while the specific gravity was tested and declared to be almost without fault. Thirteen was a good reading, but no sooner had it been taken than it was disparaged. The villagers feared The Evil Eye, the supposed power which some people had to cause harm with a look or by passing a complimentary remark but which you could also bring down on yourself by self-congratulation. Aristides opted for an each-way bet and called on the powerful chemistry of metabisulphate for help. He tipped a bag of the bacteria-zapping white powder into the *patateri* and the fumes that immediately billowed forth provoked paroxysms of gasping and spluttering from the treaders, who evacuated their posts and sought relief in cigarettes.

The acrid fumes faded and the treaders returned – to a new hazard: wasps. The sweet, sticky must had attracted them. We were now treading grapes, snail shells, which we threw out when we saw them, and wasps. Nektarios got stung and retired hurt to join the spectators. He was replaced by Aristides' son, Yiannis, and two of his school-friends, one of whom spoke to me in perfect American-English. "Where are you from?" I asked in surprise. He looked at me as if it was a daft question. "Afrata," he answered. The wasps caused only that one casualty, squashed grapes being more appealing to them than human flesh. The grapes had been well trodden once and the skins and stalks were now piled up in a corner. Georgis put a large wooden board on top of this pile and we all stood on it and jiggled about to squeeze out the very last drop of the valuable must. We had finished our work but the process was not yet complete. So far, we had produced nearly a thousand litres of what would develop over the months into a palatable, light and fruity wine with a distinct rosé character. Georgis blocked the drain hole again, raked out the skins and stalks until they were level across the *patateri* and then poured back some of the must. This would be left to steep overnight and then Georgis would give the mixture one last tread, drain it off and add it, along with some of Petrula's *petimezi*, to the previous day's must. The remaining squashed skins and stalks would then be salvaged for making *tschikoudia* at the village still and the *patateri* hosed out and handed over to its owner.

Sticky-footed and exhausted we all went back to eat the food prepared by Petrula and her daughters-in-law. The post-treading lunch was an excuse to drink the vintage wines of previous years. The Platsakis family had redefined "home-made wine" for me. Aristides clinked his glass against mine, but this time I got in first: "Aristidi! *Bomba!*" Everybody started clinking glasses and the toasts rattled around the table. It was another family feast of excellent food. Petrula only ever bought bread and a few items from the greengrocer or the supermarket in Kolymbari. Everything else was the family's own produce. Even the salt was collected from pans on the seashore. Aristides enjoyed hunting and his favourite addition to the family table was wild hare, one of which was here now, dark and delicious. Petrula had also put out plates of her own rabbit and in front of me sat an alleged delicacy – a toothy little bunny-skull. I stared at it. Nektarios leaned across the table and asked, "Don't you want that?" I shook my head and he took it. "Best bit!" he said, crunching away. "Do you like snails?" he laughingly enquired. Fortunately, they weren't on the menu but, when the rains came, they would be.

Tula asked Susan why we wanted to come and live in Crete. It was obviously a question that needed answering. Susan replied with some truths, that it was a beautiful place with a good climate and friendly people. Kyriacos leaned across. "Not all Cretans are nice, you know. Some are awful," he said. "Really?" Susan answered, anxious to learn more about the darker side of Cretan life. "Yes, in Sfakia..." he began, but Petrula interrupted him: "They're alright in Sfakia – if you don't provoke them!" "Hmmm!" grunted Kyriacos.

After my experience of choking on the metabisulphate, I wanted to know if the family used any other chemicals. After all, one of the reasons that we were leaving rural Kent was that the area was bombarded with such stuff. I remembered the first time I had experienced the problem there. I was hanging out some washing, behind the cottage, with acres of our own land all around me, and it started to rain – or so I thought. I looked up at a clear blue sky and felt my face grow damp. Puzzled, I searched for the answer – and spotted, in a nearby field, a tractor with huge "wings" on either side spraying something which the breeze was carrying back over our property... We certainly didn't want to come to Crete to live and breathe chemicals, noxious or otherwise. Anyway, Kyriacos was quite specific: he was a born-again sprayer, but only of his olives. His grapes received a scattering of Bordeaux mixture and that was all. "I spray my olives every month," he declared. "Before pesticides became available, lots of the olive trees were pest-ridden and diseased olives could be seen rotting on the ground. Many of these were collected and pressed along with the healthy ones picked from the trees. People were producing oil from mouldy olives! You're wrong to think that that 'organic' oil tasted better. It didn't," he insisted. Fortunately, this revelationary conversation did have its upsides: first, it appeared that in most cases trees were not sprayed *en masse* but were dealt with individually – by a man with a flamethrower-type can on his back and usually smoking a cigarette for protection! – and, secondly, Kyriacos said that the villagers still produced a lot of their vegetables, meat and animal products, by choice, organically.

The ruins of two hand-operated olive mills, complete with machinery, could still be seen in Afrata; one of them had already been offered to us. Kyriacos explained that the arrival of water for agricultural irrigation increased olive yields to such an extent that the old village mills could no longer cope and the work shifted to Kolymbari, where today they pressed, and processed, all the olives from miles around and exported the oil all over the world as a premium product. I had actually seen highly priced bottles of Kolymbari olive oil on the shelves of our local village store back home in Kent. Kyriacos spluttered with indignation when we told him what his oil cost in England. Apparently, the olive-growers of Afrata didn't see very much of that money and it was only the Euro-subsidies that made growing the crop worthwhile. Which was strange, because Cretan olive oil was generally agreed to be one of the world's best.

With the exception of yoghurt, you will not find much in the way of Greek foodstuffs on British supermarket shelves. It's a similar situation with history. It's Ancient Greece that pulls in the visitors; the rest of the country's past receives scant attention. Take these old olive mills, for example. A derelict windmill in England would long since have been reborn as another halt on the well-trodden "heritage" trail offering tourists an "experience" of Britain's rich agricultural and industrial past – with tea and carrot cake at exorbitant prices and, more likely than not, minuscule portions of "souvenir" fudge packaged in bags made to look like miniature sacks of flour. So far, all the olive mills that I've seen have been in worse condition than the Parthenon after Turkish gunpowder blew its roof off in 1687. Of course, I hope they stay that way! I don't want to live in a theme park where what happened in the past gets a make-over so that some fudge-merchant can exploit it as an opportunity to flog his wares to souvenir-starved day-trippers.

Kyriacos brought the conversation back to wine by asking if we were going into Hania on Monday. We were and so he asked us if we would take a sample of the new must to their *oinologos* for testing. The *oinologos* is a much-respected professional in Crete, somewhat on a par with a Harley Street consultant. The *oinologos* is a wine specialist; he analyses samples, makes a diagnosis of any problems, issues prescriptions for treatment and dispenses any necessary additives. One of his most common instructions was for the addition of extra sugar in the form of the super-sweet *petimezi*. I saw that Petrula had made quite a lot of it, but it wasn't all for the wine. Some would be eaten as a sweet-treat, topped with sesame seeds, and some would be bottled for winter use – as a cough medicine!

In the evening we walked along the wide expanse of Kolymbari's pebbly beach and realised that we would probably be wine-treading again in the morning...

Sunday with the Dagounakis started with a lurching ride in a trailer towed by their son-in-law's tractor. We were in at the beginning, picking the grapes. Eight adults, who included our lawyer, Marianna, and four children had the vines stripped within a couple of hours. The sunlight playing on the mound of freshly-picked bunches of grapes in the trailer called for an artist's palette. There were subtle mixes of alizarin crimson with French ultramarine, lemon yellow and permanent rose and Naples yellow with cobalt blue... It was an inspiring scene. Dimitra arrived with several other people, who, having turned up too late to help with the harvest, stayed to share in the impressionistic picnic that she had prepared for the vineyard labourers and which was enjoyed in *Le Déjeuner sur l'Herbe*-style – with clothes on. Because we were sitting in the shade of an olive grove, Susan seized the opportunity of comparing notes and asked Yiannis what he thought about the local olive oil in the days before pesticides. "Ah! It was wonderful!" he exclaimed. "It looked good, it smelt good and it was delicious. It was far less acidic than today's stuff – it didn't bite the back of your throat like it does now. People would die for the taste of it!" Obviously, Yiannis and Kyriacos didn't see eye-to-eye on this one. Susan hazarded another question: "What about pests in those days?" Yiannis warmed to his topic. "Well, first of all, if you didn't water your trees, the olives shrank and became less vulnerable, but we also had a spray which we made ourselves from a plant extract mixed with a tiny bit of *arseniko*," he explained. "Arsenic!" exclaimed Susan. "It was only a very little," Yiannis chuckled. One of Yiannis's grandsons asked what it was like to work in an old olive mill. Casting his mind back more than 50 years to when Afrata had last had one in operation, Yiannis recalled that a donkey had first turned two great circular mill-stones between which the fresh olives were ground into a paste. This was then packed into pillowcase-like bags woven from goat hair. Exactly 24 of these bags had then to be stacked in a huge vertical press, which demanded the strength of six men to screw down hard enough for the oil to run out. The remains were then salvaged and sent elsewhere to be processed for use in soap-making. Yiannis was one of those people students long to meet. He was a living history book!

Back at the house, the grapes were tipped into the Dagounakis's own *patateri*, which sat just outside their front gate. The experience was now familiar to us, with just one or two differences. First, Yiannis frowned on the idea of sprinkling metabisulphate powder over the grapes, which was a blessing; he always added the chemical in tablet form to his enormous barrel. Secondly, Yiannis's son, Georgis, was a confirmed rubber-boot man. Otherwise, it was the same jolly, squelchy, eating and drinking experience. There was plenty to eat, before, during and after the treading. The day ended with a Brueghel-like peasant scene in which Dimitra providing a feast of boiled mutton – and, thank the Lord, other things – for more than 30 people, some of whom had actually got their feet wet! I began to realise that these wine-treadings were actually social events that attracted more hungry and thirsty spectators than "squelchers".

It was Monday and we were in Hania. *En route* to the office of our civil engineer and architect, we stopped off at the *oinologos*, who received us in his consulting-room-cum-laboratory. Appointments were apparently unnecessary. Half-a-dozen moustachioed Cretans were hovering about in the reception area, clutching their specimen bottles. We stood with them but looked so out of place that the white-coated *oinologos* made straight for us. He knew Kyriacos and his sons well; his father had been their *oinologos* before him. He took our sample, labelled it and passed it back to one of his alchemical lab-assistants who was surrounded by the esoteric blown-glass apparatus of a Dr Frankenstein, most of it bubbling away. I could identify a Bunsen burner and a test tube but after that it was all science fantasy to me. The *oinologos* told us to call back for the results of the examination.

Dimitris, our engineer, greeted us with the offer of Greek coffee. Obviously untroubled by thoughts of The Evil Eye, he said that he made excellent coffee. Greeks take their coffee-drinking seriously and are always ready with a recommendation for one brand or another but I never found this to be very helpful because coffee is so much a matter of personal taste that one person's elixir is another's abomination. I like the relatively inexpensive Manolikakis factory-sealed brand, but a freshly roasted and ground coffee from one of the many specialist shops is unbeatable – if you can find one that you like. The problem is that the search requires you to drink a lot of coffee, some of which will be direly dusty. Nikos, the architect, arrived just as Dimitris's coffee was ready and he amazed us by executing a drinking technique that we had last seen performed by a flamingo at London Zoo. The cup was on the edge of a high table. Nikos bent down from the waist and – no hands! – slurped the froth from the top of the coffee. He repeated this two or three times before finishing off in the more usual manner. Later, in private, I tried it for myself. It was very uncomfortable and I resolved to stick with convention and lift the cup to my lips.

Nikos showed us his "roughs" for a house with a courtyard on a 200 square-metre site. Building regulations meant that two of the elevations had to be without windows. Inevitably, it was rather box-like and we said we needed time to think about it. Dimitris took the opportunity to give us a guided tour of the expensive paperwork involved in getting a building permit. In addition to the architect's regular plan and elevation drawings, there had to be detailed drawings showing how the construction would conform to the latest standards for withstanding the shock of an earthquake. Separate studies, with drawings, would be needed for the initial excavation of the site, for plumbing, drainage, septic-tank construction, insulation, electrical wiring and fireproofing. Then there would have to be quantity surveys for concrete, iron reinforcing rods and bricks. There would also be a list of the officially estimated minimum costs for each type of building work. Receipts, showing that VAT had been paid for at least these minimum sums, had to be submitted before the electricity could be connected. This was another tax office scheme to enforce payment of taxes; it would be very difficult to cut costs by getting work done "on the side", without VAT. Dimitris held up a black-covered file nearly as thick as the Canterbury telephone directory and said: "This is a standard application for building permission. Of course, you wouldn't be able to obtain it until you'd registered with IKA..." IKA? Dimitris explained that anyone building a house had to pay an agreed sum of workers' "national insurance" contributions to IKA, the Greek Department of Social Security, whether or not they employed anyone! There was a table of payments related to the size of the building and even if you did all the work yourself – in the evenings and at weekends – you'd still have to foot this bill. The fines for non-compliance were heavy. This was an unexpected expense, and it eventually added about 10% to our total building costs.

The file's journey through the bureaucratic maze would then begin with an appearance before an architectural committee, which would decide whether the design was "appropriate" for the village. This was bizarre. Even with nobbled judges, Afrata would never win a competition as Crete's most picturesque village. An allotment shed built from rusty corrugated iron, plastic sheeting and old packing cases might be "inappropriate" on the village square but it probably wouldn't raise one local eyebrow. Next in line was the Forestry Commission, which had to agree that the building would not destroy any mature tree. There was little danger of this. If any such thing, other than a crop-producing tree, of course, hadn't already been chopped or burnt down then the sheep and goats had eaten it. The procedural conveyor belt then deposited the file with the archaeologists, who would have to certify the site shard-free of potential interest. With these three boxes ticked, the file made a slow progression around the desks of various officials in the planning department, where it languished in the doldrums for a few weeks before being rubber-stamped back into life as a full-blown building permit – issued in triplicate and charged for accordingly.

"Is all that really necessary?" a dismayed Susan asked. Dimitris's answer was blunt: "Yes." We had heard that some people built without permission and saved themselves a lot of time and money. Dimitris agreed, but warned that the penalties were severe – if you got caught. It was a big "if". There were only a handful of building inspectors for the whole of western Crete and they were rumoured to be without official transport. You would have to be unlucky to get caught, and even then unlucky only in your choice of neighbours. Unless someone snitched to the authorities, you'd get away with it, more likely than not. I mused on this and Dimitris was obviously reading my mind. "Antoni, you should get a building permit. You're a foreigner and there's a risk someone might report you. For a house like yours, the authorities would fine you a million drachmas. Afterwards, you'd still have to apply for a building permit in the usual way..." We told him that we'd take the legal route, but later we came across so many people, Greeks and foreigners, who had flouted the law and got away with it that we came to regret our decision. One permit-less housebuilder we met had actually been punitively fined – but claimed that he had never been asked to pay up! He finished his house without interruption and lived happily in it, frequently enjoying a chuckle at the fitful ways of Greek bureaucracy. Of course, having paid out for a permit ourselves and followed every building regulation to the letter, we found it difficult to share in his delight. Maybe, when the next earthquake hits and shoddy, unregulated walls like his come tumbling down, he'll see that there's some merit in the system.

We returned to the *oinologos*, where Kyriacos's results were waiting for us. The *oinologos* handed us a sheet of paper identical to an NHS doctor's prescription, both in size and illegibility. "Is it alright?" Susan asked anxiously. "It's going to be fine," came the soothing answer, in exactly the same bedside-manner tone that might have been used to say, "It's a boy..." Back in Afrata, Kyriacos smiled as he read the arcane hieroglyphics of the *oinologos's* report but, still watchful of The Evil Eye, he shrugged his shoulders and grunted, "I dare say it'll make good vinegar..."

We returned to Kolymbari for our last night in Crete. Tomorrow we would be back in Kent at Gypsy Court. I had bought a book to read on the journey. It was a classic volume about the war: *The Cretan Runner* by George Psychoundakis. It was exactly what we were beginning to feel like doing – a Cretan runner! Perhaps one foggy night we could just abandon Gypsy Court in the middle of a sea of sprouts and, like the crew of the *Marie Celeste*, mysteriously disappear. Unfortunately, our elephantine building society probably never forgets its mortgagees and, like the Mounties, always gets it man. We weren't victims of negative equity but nevertheless previous marriages had bequeathed us a larger-than-healthy mortgage debt, which would, of course, have to be cleared before we could leave England. It was a satisfying thought that in Crete we wouldn't need a mortgage!

CHAPTER ELEVEN

On most charter planes, the in-flight entertainment comes on a little plastic tray and masquerades as a three-course restaurant meal. The only vaguely refreshing item I've ever found on my tray is the "flannel" impregnated with cheap cologne. On our plane home there were people tucking-in to their airline grub – and asking for more! This was their lucky day because they could have ours. Susan had prepared a picnic, which we set out on our cantilevered tabletops as the stewardess began moving down the aisle distributing meal-trays as if they were Frisbees. Two trays hovered above our heads as she stared down at the various Greek delicacies we had set out. "I don't blame you!" she said, before dishing our trays into two other laps. I don't know why the airlines bother with this charade; a plate of fresh sandwiches, cut from decent bread of course, would be better received.

Pug and Mavros were overjoyed to see us. In fact, rather noisily so. During their sojourn at the kennels they had been eating an experimental brand of dried food and were now in a perpetual state of flatulence. Pug, the senior and more dignified of the pair, was burbling dreadfully, making a bubbling noise just like someone under-water saying, "What-about-a-hot-water-bottle?" Every time he did this, he looked ponderously over his shoulder, like a fusty old solicitor with half-moon specs. I thought he was trying to shift the blame on to Mavros, who would generally be sitting behind him when this happened. Mavros countered by sniffing the air like a tracker dog and then ostentatiously recoiling from his reeking friend. This was unusual for him; a good, strong pong had always seemed to be his idea of paradise. Unlike Pug, who liked to stand, Mavros preferred to break wind while lying down. You'd see him take a deep breath and then a sort of shuddering noise would issued forth from one end, to be followed by a satisfied sigh from the other. Susan, her nose screwed up in horror, said, "All we want now is for the farmer to start!" "The farmer? He lives miles away!" I exclaimed. Susan explained that she was referring to his crop of sprouts. I had to agree; malodorous months of rotting brassica *and* flatulent pugs posed a serious threat to the sale of the house. Only people with completely bunged-up nostrils would even consider buying. We immediately switched the dogs back to their usual food, but nothing was ever going to be the same again; they continued to break wind frequently. When they actually started farting contrapuntally and *fortepiano* we christened our two canine trombonists "The Whoopee Cushions" and thought about looking for a recording contract.

We had returned to Gypsy Court to discover that there had been a murder in the locality. Although the horrendous crime had not been committed anywhere near our cottage, and we did not know the victim, the tragedy touched our life. The estate agent reported that offers he had received on houses in the area were being withdrawn and our house, which was in an isolated position, would now be that much harder to sell. We would have to wait until the memory of this dreadful event faded – or someone came from elsewhere, unaware of what had happened. "It's not the sort of thing I'd chat to prospective purchasers about if I were you," he advised, rather unnecessarily. A hint of autumn's nip was already in the air and we knew that we were in for a long winter.

Why did we buy Gypsy Court? More to the point, why wouldn't anyone else buy it now? I had seen it a few years earlier after a Canterbury estate agent sent a batch of details to our house in Kennington, in south London, where we lived in a small, virtually detached, lodge-type house, built just before the first world war in the "Regency revival" style. When we had bought that house, the agent referred to the owner, lightly, as if we might have heard of him, as "Prince Charles". The house being where it was, almost in Brixton, I thought that the seller might perhaps be a rap musician whose reputation had fortunately passed me by, but no, it was *The* Prince Charles. The house was a Duchy of Cornwall property, built on land once owned by the Black Prince, and the registered owner was HRH himself. It had been tenanted by a policeman who had done his duty at Buckingham Palace, but now he had gone and these empty "grace-and-favour" places were being sold off. Prince Charles did not show us around, but nevertheless, we liked his house, made him an acceptable offer and eventually signed a contract in which one whole page was filled up with the prince's full name and titles – against which the prosaic "Anthony John Cox & Susan Margaret Forbes" came as an anticlimax. Like all houses, it had its good and bad points. The neighbours spoke, well most of them did, it was very convenient for the City and the West End and we still had a few good shops on our doorstep. Against this, the streets around were noisy, dirty and violent – and Lambeth was the notorious local council. After our house was burgled and our new car destroyed by passing incendiarists, our enthusiasm for inner-city life dipped. When we were abusively threatened by a woman we found peeing in *our* front doorway, we decided to find somewhere less eventful to live. We thought that life would somehow be "kinder" in the countryside and Gypsy Court – on offer as a thatched cottage "with potential" *and* six acres of land – was irresistible, not least because there were no other houses nearby. We bought it, in retrospect rather too easily, and the prince's old house was sold quickly enough to a young City gent. We were glad to leave Kennington but, much to our surprise, our departure did not go unmarked. Dave Isaacs, our local real-meat butcher, gave us his solid old English beechwood chopping block, which had fallen foul of Eurocratic foodshop laws, as a farewell present. "Butcher Dave" should have had a conservation order slapped on him; he was a kind-hearted chirpy Londoner of the old school who delighted in making friends with his customers and being of service to them. We were particularly sad to be saying goodbye to his excellent boned-and-rolled sirloin!

The Rattue family had occupied Gypsy Court for more than 50 years, since before the war. Harry Rattue described to us how in 1940 he had watched the Battle of Britain from the garden and seen the bombing of Canterbury from his bedroom window. He had run the place as a smallholding but now he was ill and wanted to move away. Susan had had experience of restoring an old cottage – in Dorset – and she sensed that this one was still intact behind layers of modern "improvements", which consisted mainly of pink-painted hardboard sheeting. She turned out to be right; underneath all the hardboard, Gypsy Court was still as it had been in 1794. Unfortunately, although the local conservation officer complimented us on our restoration work, he wouldn't let us extend the cottage beyond one extra room, so we were stuck with a large kitchen-dining room, a small utility room, a small living room, a corkscrew of a staircase, one medium-sized bedroom, one small bedroom and a bathroom. There were some old agricultural outbuildings of the cement-block variety – and six acres of land on which we couldn't build anything except a future as cabbage-growers.

The cottage was cramped and so was our life-style; we couldn't put out all of our books nor find enough wall-space for our pictures. The flat landscape was monotonous – and we had no neighbours, which was appealing at first, but soon emphasised our sense of isolation. The surrounding villages were well-swept, well-mown lifeless places inhabited by commuters or retired bungalow-dwelling townies – and a few "locals" who seldom condescended to acknowledge in-comers like us. Not once did I see a straw-chewing yokel leaning on a five-bar gate cheerfully delivering rural wit and wisdom to passers-by. That may have been because in east Kent rural wit and wisdom went out with the horse-and-plough, but it could have been because there weren't any passers-by. None of the pavement-less country lanes were safe to walk on. The inadequacy of public transport made a reliable car an expensive necessity for virtually everyone and this meant that the narrow, winding lanes were always busy with speeding traffic – most of it mothers frenetically driving around in circles juggling busy schedules of dropping-off and picking-up. Near-misses were all too frequent as these stressed-out unpaid family taxi-drivers hurled their cars around blind blends in a desperate attempt to get to the school gates before the bell. Slow-moving agricultural vehicles also contributed to the problem; long tail-backs of cars formed in the lanes and the pent-up fury of drivers forced to crawl along at 10 mph was a force to be avoided. When it rained, which it did often, farm tractors chewed up the road verges and splattered everything with slippery mud. The roads also iced up at the drop of a thermometer and the wind was fierce; indoors, the winter heating bills were huge. There were summer days, sitting with friends from London in the cottage garden, when it did seem idyllic but the feeling never lasted. We knew we'd made a mistake and when we discovered that despite his 50-plus years at Gypsy Court several "locals" we spoke to couldn't place the name of the previous owner, we resolved to leave. There was no point in working hard to find the money to pay the bills to stay in a place we didn't like and which it seemed would never get to like us. In truth, there was more human contact in an inner-London suburb, but a return to Kennington was out of the question. We thought again about Scotland and about Cornwall and Devon, those western counties of in-comers and carved-up, asset-stripped old rural properties, but decided against them. That's really where our Cretan story began.

Gypsy Court was having another effect on us: its six acres of open land emphasised the smallness of our plot in Afrata. Two hundred square metres just wasn't big enough; the house would take up most of the space, leaving us with nothing more than a courtyard to serve as a garden. Had we been impulsive? "You can't live with a view," I told Susan, rather late in the day. She agreed that I was rather late in coming to that conclusion and claimed credit for pointing out the limitations of the site from the moment we first saw it. I didn't remember her saying anything, but there was no point in arguing. We tried looking at those 200 square metres as 2,153 square feet, but it didn't make any difference. Metric or imperial, the plain truth was that our site was just too small. Reluctantly, Susan telephoned the civil engineer and the architect and told them not to do any more work on preparing plans for a house. Now we were just the owners of a stone-and-rubble shack in western Crete. Perhaps we could sell it? The thought of asking someone like the "medallion man" agent to find a buyer stirred us to more positive thoughts. We decided to return to Afrata to see if we could buy some of the adjacent land.

Direct flights from London to Hania are only available for about half the year; outside the holiday season you have to fly to Athens and then take one of the all-year-round Athens-Hania domestic flights. It's a toss-up as to which is worse. Greeks are the world's pushiest travellers and they'll elbow aside anyone who gets in their way. They won't queue or extend the simplest of common courtesies to a fellow traveller; it's standard behaviour for them to shove, barge, jab and shout their way from start to finish – and to blow cigarette smoke over you whenever they can. It's either that or a plane-load of drunken holiday-making Brits yelling "Viva Espana!" Of course, some people do the journey by car and ferry but that extrudes the misery from about three hours to nearly a week. Robert Louis Stevenson may have thought it better to travel hopefully than to arrive, but he died before he had the chance to experience air travel.

We arrived in Hania in the middle of a December rainstorm. We stayed for a week and it rained every day. It's a political joke that Russia has only two seasons – spring and winter; it's a plain fact that in Crete if it's not summer, it's winter. Springtime and autumn hardly exist in the English sense, although those months are slightly milder and comfortable for travelling around. In summer it's hot and dry and in the winter any meteorologist will confirm that there's "abundant precipitation". The closeness of Africa can make December afternoons on Crete's southern coast like those of a northern-European summer day, but in the north of the island it's just as likely to be wet – and often windy. A shepherd with a crook in one hand and an old-fashioned black umbrella in the other is a common winter sight. The rain falls as snow on the high mountain peaks. Yiannis Dagounakis can remember snow falling around Afrata back in 1927 and again in 1972. The truth is that for the English, a place like Afrata never gets that cold. The villagers complain bitterly, don woolly hats and wrap themselves in scarves and thick coats, but they have no conception of what it means to be really cold. You have to live through a winter on the English east coast for that! It's wet, very wet – and can be for days on end – that's the distinctive feature of the Cretan winter.

The rain that greeted our arrival also delayed our first night's sleep. We had rented a furnished flat in Astratigos, the sepulchral village next-door to Afrata. The flat was one of two "holiday homes" converted from an old house. We were downstairs and we had been told that there were Germans upstairs. There are Germans everywhere in Crete so this did not surprise us. The rain had got heavier and was noisily lashing at the wooden window-shutters, which had all been battened down. We were snug in bed but we could hear the sound of rushing water. We thought it was running down the hill outside. Suddenly, upstairs erupted with guttural barks and hysterical shrieks. These were soon accompanied by the noise of banging doors – and gushing water. It was like the soundtrack from a war-film, where a depth charge has just breached the hull of a U-boat and the frenzied crew are desperately trying to save themselves. The same frenzy was obviously occurring upstairs, where there was now the sound of frantic sloshing about with orders being excitedly yelled every which way. It was as good as a war-at-sea film! The noise stopped as abruptly as it had begun. They were either all dead upstairs or, like skilful submariners, they'd eventually got the watertight hatches firmly shut. The following morning we saw one of the Germans, who explained that their flat had a large, walled balcony-cum-terrace, which the heavy rain had filled up like a water-tank because the drain-hole had got blocked. Eventually, the water breached the door into the flat and the pent-up gallons cascaded in. "Unfortunately, the balcony is a lot higher than the floor of the flat," explained the German. I made a mental note to build rain-protection into any house of ours.

Later that morning, carrying our umbrellas, we went calling on people in Afrata. It was now too cold and wet for the two *kafenea*-keepers to maintain their lookout for potential customers so no shouts greeted our arrival in the village. We went first to see Kyriacos and Petrula, who were sitting around a primitive wood-burning stove which had a large flue pipe going up to the ceiling and then snaking overhead across the room before disappearing through a hole knocked in the wall. This temporary fitting would be dismantled in the summer. They greeted us warmly and served us coffee – and *tschikoudia*. We asked them about the land immediately in front of our plot. This brought a chuckle from Kyriacos. "I think you'll find it has a lot of owners," he said. What he meant by this wasn't quite clear, but it seemed that trying to buy it would be fraught with difficulty, of that much Kyriacos was certain. We left them and headed for the Dagounakis house, on our way passing the path leading to the Asteri *kafeneon*.

Stephania spotted us and insisted that we had coffee with her. Fortunately, Greek coffees are small! Her *kafeneon* was heated by another of these crudely-made but effective wood-stoves. Hers, however, had three times more meandering and temporary flue pipe indoors than Kyriacos's contraption. She had news: the olive mill had been sold – to a German. However, nothing in Afrata is ever straightforward. It transpired that the German lived in Israel and he'd be coming to live in the village with his daughter, who was Swiss... I asked Stephania a question that I had not thought to ask before: "Are there any foreigners in the village?" Apparently, there were about ten Bulgarians living in the old school-building, two Frenchwomen and a German couple with holiday homes, an Englishman ditto, an American couple, whose son I'd met while grape-treading – and, down in the lower village, a Kurd and two English holiday-homers. So we weren't the only ones.

We walked up to Turnip's old stable before calling on Yiannis and Dimitra. The fields around now looked much greener than they had a few months ago. There wasn't much of a view through the steadily falling rain, but we still liked what we saw. Although the air was fresh, it wasn't cold. It was like the English West Country or the Lakes, except that here the weather didn't seem to penetrate one's bones. Yiannis didn't altogether agree. We met him on his way down from the mountain, where his sheep had been grazing. He was dressed in army-surplus rubberised waterproofs like someone headed for the trenches; his headgear was a close-fitting leather pilot's helmet with earflaps, he had a tartan muffler round his neck and he was wearing heavy-duty knee-high leather boots. He also had a huge, multi-coloured golfing umbrella. After a rapid greeting he launched into a condemnation of the awful weather. We thought it was quite acceptable, but diplomacy required us to agree with him. He looked at our little folding umbrellas and thin anoraks, shook his head and tut-tutted. "Come! Let's go to the house," he said.

After a nip of *tschikoudia*, Yiannis obviously felt better. Through the window I saw a black umbrella slowly moving across the courtyard, apparently by itself. Dimitra opened the door and the umbrella collapsed to reveal a tiny Antonia, swathed in layers of black winter-clothing and with another variant of the eccentric turban-like headgear we had seen her wearing many months earlier. She welcomed us as if we'd last seen her only yesterday and then took a seat next to a fumy oil-burning stove that made the whole room smell like an old-fashioned English ironmonger's shop. We discussed everybody's health, which wasn't such a good idea because they all claimed to be dying from various ills. This led to a summary of the funerals there had been in the past month or so. Thinking there had to be more to life in Afrata than this, I mentioned the sale of the olive-mill to a German. Yiannis began shaking his head, but Antonia suddenly said, "They came up here and threw all our things out of the house and into the yard." Susan gave me a puzzled glance. "Who did that?" she asked Antonia. "The German soldiers," explained the old lady. "They came up here and took anything they wanted. If they couldn't find anything, they got angry. If they'd have just left us alone, we wouldn't have taken any notice of them at all." This was too much for Yiannis, who still suffered from the injuries he sustained trying to keep the Germans out of Crete and before that, halting the Italian advance in Albania, where many Greek soldiers were disabled by frostbite – caused mainly, said Yiannis, by the tight puttees the right-wing Metaxas government ordered its troops to wear. According to the old soldier, the heroic Greek troops were virtually shot in the feet by their leaders and were disabled from subsequently fighting the real enemy: the Germans. Anyway, whatever he said to Antonia was unintelligible to us because he had reverted to their Cretan dialect. Antonia hugged herself and seemed to become even smaller; a flap from her turban dropped down over her forehead and she began muttering under her breath. In contrast, Yiannis's voluble indignation seemed to make him expand. Dimitra brought the subject to an end by declaring that lunch was ready. I looked up at the clock; they were a little late today – it was 11.05. "You'll stay?" she invited. This should have been our cue to leave but we couldn't because we hadn't yet asked about the land around our plot. "Thank you," said Susan.

We moved into the kitchen, our hair and clothes well-impregnated with kerosene fumes. Antonia stayed sitting by the stove, still muttering to herself. Lunch in the cold and draughty kitchen consisted of shrivelled olives that looked like black tiger-nuts, a plate of cold fish and a bowl of cold *horta* in olive oil. If Yiannis had complained of the cold, I would have sincerely agreed with him. The hardy Dagounakis couple heated only their living room. I realised a truth about these old stone-built Cretan houses – in winter, they were cold, damp and draughty. I was glad that we had let go of the dream of restoring a picturesque old ruin. That thought brought the reason for our visit to the fore. The mention of land led Dimitra to leave the table and check that the door was properly shut. Her voice dropped to a whisper. The piece of land that wrapped itself around two sides of our stable belonged to Antonia's brother. "Well, that's good. We can ask her if he'd like to sell it," I said. This provoked a lecture from Yiannis.

"Slowly, slowly, Antoni," he said, wagging his finger. He set out the general principles of land-purchase in Crete. In the end it seemed that there was only one rule, an iron one: Don't Ask. If people don't want to sell land, they won't; if they do want to sell, they'll approach anyone who might want to buy. "If you wait, they will come to you. If you start asking, they'll have the upper hand and you'll have pay more than you need to," he warned. This wasn't very encouraging. Susan asked if they thought that Antonia's brother might want to sell his land. Dimitra answered, "He might..." Yiannis brought the discussion to an end with another little bout of finger-wagging: "Slowly, slowly, Antoni."

Antonia had already returned to her house next door when we left. We decided to call on her. Her kitchen-cum-living room could have garaged four cars but this barn-like place was heated only by a device that looked like a dustbin-lid on legs. It was a *mangali*, a shallow brazier holding charcoal and other smouldering bits and pieces. The fumes were noxious and in a more confined space would have been lethal. The warmth radiated for about a metre, after that it was cold. Antonia insisted on making coffee for us and like all old ladies everywhere she also had a tin of damp biscuits for her visitors. It's impossible to visit a Cretan home without being offered something to eat or drink! We wanted to ask about her brother's land but our around-the-houses conversation couldn't get us anywhere near the subject. Eventually, Susan asked Antonia about her family. Antonia seized the opportunity to start another conversation on the subject of poor health. "My brother Antonis is in Athens. He's very unwell – and it's an expensive business being ill..." she sighed. This wasn't quite what we had expected to hear, but it gave a glimmer of hope that her brother might think about selling his land. Propped up in a glass-fronted cabinet was a recent photograph of an elderly man. "Is that your brother?" I asked. Antonia confirmed that it was. "Slowly, slowly" may be good advice but sometimes time is against you. I asked her about the piece of land behind the mule's stable. "It belongs to my brother," she answered, but a barely perceptible change in her expression showed that she had become alert to a possibility...

CHAPTER TWELVE

We had lit the blue touch paper; now we had to wait and see. Our tiny plot of land was on a corner site, its dry-stone walls bounded on two sides by rough tracks – each as wide as a donkey loaded with two panniers – and on its other flanks by Antonia's brother's land, in the middle of which grew a huge and ancient almond tree. The scrubby land to the front of our plot, across one of the tracks, would be useful as a garden – after much preparatory work – but the other piece of land, with its stretches of fertile red earth, was a much more attractive proposition. We were ready to take things "slowly, slowly" – but not for too long.

The name of the village where we were staying – Astratigos – meant "without a general"; the place seemed to be without nearly everything else as well. There was a part-time *kafeneon* tucked away in a back street, two churches – one of them of recent construction, a few ruined buildings and a few new or refurbished ones. A human being was an uncommon sight. The village, however, had at least two things going for it: it was quiet, in fact, it was deathly so at times, and it was a place from which you could happily ramble freely in any direction. The surrounding rocky countryside offered rough hill-walking or the promise of steadier progress on a network of unmade agricultural tracks, in which deep, muddy puddles were now forming. In winter, one walked for fresh air and exercise but in the Cretan spring, there was always a profusion of wild flowers to be enjoyed – and bird-watchers could spot a good number of resident or migratory species. Now it was December, but we could still see some late-flowering deep reddish-pink cyclamen – probably the common *Cyclamen graecum* – around us as we walked over the wet hills. A number of species of cyclamen can be found on Crete, including the long-lived *Cyclamen hederifolium*, which can last for a 100 years. There were also birds to be seen, but, not being "twitchers", we probably couldn't have identified them, even if we had had our binoculars with us. Crete, although 35 times smaller, is almost as well-endowed with flora as Britain – the island has more than 2,000 species of plants, 130 of them endemic – but when you've taken away the birds, the fauna's a bit thin on the ground. The wild goat, the *kri-kri*, is a very rare sight, having been hunted to the point of extinction, and we've only ever seen the ones kept in captivity in the public gardens in Hania. However, the bushy-tailed, cat-sized Cretan fox, a close relative of the weasel, pops up quite frequently and bats, hares, rabbits, hedgehogs and various rodents can also be seen, along with frogs, toads and turtles – and 11 different small reptiles, all of which are harmless to humans.

Our early morning ramble brought us to a point high above Kolymbari, although the weather got in the way of the view. We decided to descend, do some shopping and return to Astratigos by taxi. In the greengrocer's we were greeted with a cry of recognition from the owner. "Ah! You're here again! How are you?" he said. I was a little taken aback by this. We had bought some fruit from him on our last visit, but that was all. "Do you recognise us?" I asked. "Of course," he said. "You were here in September and before that in the summer." We were obviously already better-known in Crete than in Kent. Were we so extraordinary? Back in Kent we had definitely merged into the foreground. I thought of the junk shop in our local village where I had bought many things and had stood and chatted with the dealer many more times than I had made purchases. After a couple of years as a regular customer, the owner of the shop owed me some money from a deal we had made but he couldn't even remember my name when he came to write out the cheque! The greengrocer told us we could pick up a taxi just across the road or outside the butcher's shop, the butchers themselves doubling-up as taxi-drivers. All the taxis were busy so we decided to wait and have coffee at a traditional old *kafeneon* near the post office. It was called "The New".

Nikos, the proprietor, was also a barber and within the *kafeneon* a single-seat parlour had been partitioned off for hair-cutting. He ran the two businesses in tandem and customers halfway through a trim might be asked to wait while he made coffee for those who wanted refreshment. The *kafeneon* was furnished with a haphazard scattering of traditional wooden tables and chairs and modern plastic garden furniture. The white-ish walls of the *kafeneon* were decorated with an antique pendulum clock, two huge bunches of onions, a TV set and five framed coloured pencil-drawings. They were masterpieces of naïve art. There were four portraits of 19th century Cretan military heroes and a double-picture showing the Church of St Sofia in Constantinople and the death, in 1453, of the last Greek ruler of the Byzantine empire. To this work, Xenophos Simantirakis, the artist, had added a caption declaring that he was self-taught and that he had completed the picture in 1970 when he was 86 years old. According to Nikos, whose predecessor at "The New" had been given the pictures by the artist, Xenophos was a fascinating character who had enjoyed a reputation as an inventor and a photographer, using a huge plate camera that he had built himself.

The *kafeneon*, with its unexpected art collection, was undoubtedly the most interesting place to be found in Kolymbari's disjointed central streets. The little harbour had been interesting when we first saw it, but it had been "improved" with cement and now looked just like a car park. The fishing boats were still there, however. Unfortunately, one couldn't say the same for the shady avenue of fine mature trees that had led from the supermarket into the village proper. They had been cleared after our first visit to make way for further "improvements", this time to the pavement. Although one guidebook makes the somewhat extravagant claim that Kolymbari is a "small and pretty village", most don't even try to find words to describe the place. I would describe the village as "small and bald" and if I had to choose a colour to capture Kolymbari's vibrancy it would be well-faded neutral tint.

The shops were mostly like the greengrocer's store: well-stocked and friendly. The village had two bakeries, one run by a Greek couple who were said to have previously owned a fish-and-chip shop in Tasmania. The first time I bought bread there, I blinked twice when I saw the words "EXOTIC ARSE" peeping out from behind a pile of sticky buns. It took another visit before I realised that this wasn't a bizarre point-of-sale gimmick to shift more buns; it was just a stray title from the shop's stock of pornographic magazines. Kolymbari was such a small and gossipy place that I couldn't imagine anyone striding into the shop and boldly demanding: "A large white loaf and this month's *Exotic Arse...*" But presumably people did! When I tried the other baker, he gave me a glass of *tschikoudia* along with my change. The most important shop in the village is undoubtedly the co-op supermarket, a dismal and scruffy place which stocks a larger range of washing-up liquids than a Tesco superstore back in England but is otherwise unremarkable. There's also a traditional tobacconist's kiosk – a *periptero* – where Susan got sharply told off for leaning on the unavoidable chewing-gum display. It's been on our blacklist ever since... Shopping in Kolymbari was obviously very different in Yiannis's day. He could remember the village from the 1930s, when it was more like a bustling town. There were seven separate shoe and boot-makers, two of them specialising in nail-studded working boots, two doctors – one of whom was also a commercial wine-producer, and several other stores both general and specialist. There were even boats sailing directly between Kolymbari and the Peloponnese.

The sprawling village boasts a long, pebbly beach, occasionally tar-spotted and not entirely free of the plastic detritus of the packaging industry. It is usually quiet, not least because Kolymbari has no really big hotels. The beach stretches a long way towards Maleme, at one point passing the broken remains of some wartime defences. Within the village, there's a string of tavernas along the water's edge but the places we liked to eat at most of all were the two fish-tavernas in the main street. The oddly-named Argentina confronts the Diktyna across the narrow road. The Diktyna has the better position, with a large balcony overlooking the sea, but the Argentina has more tables and a wider menu – and a magnificent stuffed stag's head to remind you that it's a fish-taverna. On the other hand, Dimitris Marnerakis, the Diktyna's fisherman-proprietor, catches, cooks and serves his own fish a lot of the time. The two tavernas sit on opposite sides of the road in a state of happy competition. The Argentina is well-known locally for its *kolokythopitta*, a savoury courgette-in-pastry dish, and the Diktyna for its fish soup. Between them, the two tavernas go some way towards redeeming a visit to downtown Kolymbari.

Kolymbari's outskirts have two main claims to attention: first, on the road towards Afrata, there's the Camelot-ish monastery of Gonia, where a cannon ball fired by attacking Turks in July 1867 can still be seen embedded in a wall. The monastery traces its history back to the middle of the ninth century, when there was a monastic community further north, up the peninsula beyond the village of Rodopou. Piratical depredations eventually forced the monks southwards towards Kolymbari, where in 1618 they started building on the present site. For more than 200 years they had a lot of trouble from the Turks but then, after the incident with the cannon ball, things quietened down until 1941 when the Germans invaded, took over the monastery buildings and used them as a training camp, but apparently not for the production of military chaplains. Today, it's only tourists – by coincidence, mostly German – who interrupt the pursuit of the monastic life. The monks are fighting back, however – they won't allow anyone in who's wearing shorts, including *lederhosen*.

The other place of importance is the huge modern co-operative olive oil processing plant and winery, where no one ever seems to challenge you wandering around and where the high-quality local oil and drinkable wine – red and white – can be sampled and then purchased cheaply in bulk, which is a good idea because a single bottle of co-op red wine doesn't seem to go very far.

We had finished our coffees at "The New" *kafeneon* and were just about to make another attempt at getting a taxi to take us up to Astratigos when a large four-wheel drive open-backed truck screeched to a halt in front of us. It was Aristides Platsakis in his Toyota. "How are you?" asked Aristides. Cretans always ask you this and unlike England, you're expected to reply. Not in detail; a word's enough. The most common reply, of course, is, "Fine – and you?" – but if you're feeling a little low you can say, "Medium – and you?" We told him we were fine and he replied by telling us he was in the same condition. He offered us a lift up the mountain. We saw that he already had passengers in his driving cab and I asked, "How?" He jerked his thumb over his shoulder and grinned, "Hop in the back!" We roared off up the mountain clinging on to the sides of his open truck. It was a white-knuckle experience, swaying between sea and sky, and when we came to a halt in Afrata we were glad to get off and realign our internal organs. Kyriacos was standing outside his house. "How are you?" I asked. He jiggled a gnarled hand in front of him in a so-so fashion and said, "Medium – and you?" Breaking with convention, I said that I had felt better before the ride. Kyriacos laughed and invited us in for a glass of *tschikoudia*. This is another thing that Cretans always do!

Kostis crossed the narrow road from his *kafeneon*, the Kali Kardia, and came into Kyriacos's living room. "How are you?" he asked... He poured himself a *tschikoudia* and said that he'd come to do us a favour. Susan's internal alarm bell sounded at exactly the same time as mine. We looked at each other and then at Kostis. "Yes?" we said slowly and suspiciously together. His son, Jakovos, had a house in the village and he was prepared to let part of it to us as a temporary home while we built our own place. "Thank you, but we're not yet ready to rent a home in Afrata," Susan told him. Kostis slapped the table, and said, "No problem! Jakovos's house isn't ready either!"

Just around the corner from Kyriacos and Petrula was the new but ugly three-storey building that Kostis had come to tell us about. The upper floors had been finished off and were obviously lived-in but the ground floor was just a breezeblock shell inhabited by a scruffy grey-and-black mongrel tied to a length of dirty rope. There were no doors or windows and the floor was bare concrete. Kostis called his son down to meet us. Jakovos worked on the buses, grew olives and hunted. He lived with his wife and two young children on the floors above and now wanted to finish his house by turning the ground floor into a self-contained flat. The deal was straightforward: if we would pay six months rent in advance, he would have enough money to complete the building work. We could then have the two-bedroomed flat for a year. The rent would work out at about £25 a week. Our problem, of course, was that we wouldn't be moving to Crete until Gypsy Court was sold. Jakovos shrugged his shoulders and said the rental would start when we were ready. Susan cast a critical eye over the work yet to be done. "Are you sure you'll have enough money for it?" she asked. "No problem!" replied our would-be future landlord. We promised to give him an answer the next day, but because I was beginning to acquire some Cretan habits, I added, "Or the day after…"

We walked up the road and into Astratigos. The sky was filled with scudding clouds; it would undoubtedly rain again later. Lunch beckoned and so we got in the car and drove over the unmade back road towards Kastelli for a return visit to our favourite taverna, The Stork. We ordered octopus-in-vinegar, followed by pork *stifado* – cooked with meat from one of the taverna's own pigs – pot-roast veal in brandy, *horta* and, of course, red wine from the barrel. It was all good, but the octopus was extraordinarily succulent and Susan remarked upon it to Dimitris, the Stork's proprietor. "Tender, eh?" he said. It was; too often, octopus has a rubbery quality but this had been delicious. "I put it in the cement mixer," said Dimitris blandly. Octopus has to be tenderised by vigorous bashing but most people don't bash long enough, hence the chewy texture of the octopus generally served up in tavernas. "Sticking it in the cement mixer softens it up a treat. Of course, you can use a washing machine if you like – but only on a cold cycle!" he confided.

We walked off lunch – which had cost us less than £10 and would have been much cheaper than that but for my predilection for octopus – with a stroll around the virtually deserted streets of Kastelli. All the shops were shut and it had come on to rain again. It was a drab town and but for our excellent lunch, it might have depressed us. However, in Crete, there's always something just around the next corner. In this case it was someone – the man with the botched-up house. We had a desultory conversation, which we brought to a close by claiming that a pressing engagement awaited us. As we watched him trot off, a car with GB plates drew up. An obviously English middle-aged couple got out, overheard us talking, glanced at each other, jumped back in their car – and drove off. "Maybe they saw whatsit? Or perhaps they're on the run," suggested Susan. It was a strange non-encounter. We had been ready to say a brief "hello," but, like a lot of expatriates that we encountered, this pair obviously didn't want any contact at all. British expat-types in Greece often behave like this towards their compatriots. They're very much like those distant young people who won't have unguarded social intercourse with anyone over 40 – presumably for fear of contracting "Age"! Cretans are so much more relaxed and sociable and will generally talk to anyone.

A return visit to the Rotonda was on our list. It wasn't a particularly auspicious time for visiting the church because Melkhizedek, the young monk, was quite likely to be taking a siesta. However, we had a small present for him: a photograph of St Michael and All Angels, at Lancing, near Brighton, the church where I had been baptised. It had been taken by a friend of mine – called Michael... Melkhizedek's interest in St Michael had led him to amass a collection of books, pamphlets, photographs and pictures relating to the saint – mostly sent by tourists who had enjoyed visiting the Byzantine church. The ancient church was being lashed by rain when we arrived. Its gloomy interior was still and deserted. Hesitantly, I called out: "Melkhizedek!" Some curtains parted and the monk, beaming and wide awake, came down the few steps from his cell at the back of the church. He extended his hands in a warm welcome: "Susannah! Antonis! How are you?" We sat and drank *tschikoudia* inside the cold church; I wondered what the incumbent of St Michael and All Angels served to his church-visitors in Lancing. Melkhizedek was not as happy as he had been when we first met him; there seemed to be problems with his plans to stay and keep the church open and to re-establish the monastery that had existed here under his namesake. He was thin on detail but the difficulties were obviously affecting him deeply. He perked up when I gave him the photograph. "And I have something for you, Antoni!" he said. He went to his cell and returned with an icon of St Anthony. I told him that when I built a house in Crete I would also construct a shrine and I would put the icon in there. Melkhizedek apologised to Susannah that he had nothing for her. Susan told him that she'd settle for another *tschikoudia*. It was that chilly in the church.

On our way home the rain stopped, and so did we – in Kolymbari. We made the short walk uphill, southwards past the telephone exchange and the junior school, to the older, but now absorbed, village of Grimviliana. We wanted to see the place where Xenophos Simantirakis, the naïve artist, had lived. Grimviliana was virtually indistinguishable from its undistinguished neighbour but it had retained some of its traditional Cretan charm, despite the intrusion of new buildings and heavy restoration work on others. Foreigners are everywhere in Crete and Grimviliana, named after a Turkish chieftain of old, was no exception. German, Austrian and Swiss-registered cars were parked on the small *plateia*, but much rarer birds could be heard... Grimviliana's maze of narrow alleys resounded to the raucous shouts of young Americans. German accents are so common as to be unremarkable, but it's most unusual to hear American voices so far away from the well-trodden tourist trail through ancient archaeological sites and museums. Turning a corner in the heart of the old village, we saw a youth, his baseball cap on back-to-front, come wobbling towards us on a bit of broken furniture with squeaking castors. When he saw us, he braked by swerving into a house wall. The slogans on his cap, sweatshirt and baseball jacket told us he had to be American. He flashed us a toothy grin and, like a puppy, he cheerfully barked, "Hi!" We stopped to chat. He told us that there were young Americans around and about these parts for six months every year. "And what are you doing here?" I asked. "You know, stuff. We do stuff, writing and stuff, and we work with animals and stuff..." he said. "Lots of stuff, eh?" I commented, although I was really none the wiser. "Yeah! See you!" he yelled as he pushed off on his makeshift skateboard – presumably in search of yet more stuff. A villager, passing by, noted our bafflement. "*Americanos,*" he said, as if that explained everything. I later learned, that the boy was on one of those often remedial "study abroad programs" so beloved of American parents. I must say, if I had the money and a son who said "stuff" as often as the lad we had met I'd probably pay someone to knock it out of him!

Crete's heterogeneous population is, thankfully, still predominantly Greek but the foreign language most commonly heard is German. In the hotchpotch of folk who more-or-less permanently inhabit the island, German-speaking foreigners must outnumber the combined total of other European nationalities. Crete exerts a peculiar fascination on the German-speaking peoples, which is understandable but at times bizarre. If the stories are true, it's easy to see why, for example, there are so many young-ish Germans here without any obvious means of support. Excessively generous German unemployment benefit, when converted into drachmas, comes out at a great deal more than the Cretan average wage and there are reportedly lots of Germans biding their time and enjoying a relaxed life in the sun on "imported" social security benefits. The DSS, with its regular checks and strictly-applied book of rules, certainly doesn't make a long holiday in Crete an easy option for jobless Brits – while an Albanian or Russian will think that he's enjoying social security when sitting undisturbed on a Hania park bench with his mates! As for the bizarre, I once fell into conversation, in a village *kafeneon*, with a resident middle-aged German who told me that he had come to live in Crete because his father had been very happy on the island. "Your father?" I asked. "Yes, he was here in the war with the *Wehrmacht*."

In Astratigos the next morning, we were startled to hear our names being shouted. We went to the window and there in the narrow street below the window was a man we had not seen before. He told us that he had come to talk about the land behind our mule stable. We invited him in and served *tschikoudia* – the essential Cretan lubricant in such situations – from a bottle that Yiannis had given us. As usual, we discussed matters of varying degrees of irrelevance until our visitor suddenly came to the point, telling us what we already knew: that the land wasn't his and that he was merely acting for the owner. We could have the land if we were prepared to pay the owner's asking price, which he now revealed to us. We weren't. This was a not-very-risky gamble. Based on our previous experience, it seemed to us that the first figure quoted by a seller was only ever a starting point and should always be countered with an offer lower than the price one would eventually be prepared to pay. This gave the leeway necessary for the two parties to strike a bargain acceptable to both and was the Cretan way of doing business. Our counter-offer was greeted with a deprecating sigh. This was par for the course and we did not expect matters to end there. Our visitor left after promising to talk to the land's owner. We decided that we should telephone our lawyer, Marianna, to arrange a power of attorney so that if anything came of these negotiations, she could act promptly on our behalf.

After this call, we drove down to Afrata to tell Jakovos that we had decided to accept his offer of the as yet non-existent flat. The rental arrangement was toasted, naturally enough, with *tschikoudia* and our demand that there should be a written contract was agreed to. The village had an official called "The Secretary", who operated out of the community office on the *plateia*. He was a kind of rural town clerk who could tap out an agreement for us on his mechanical typewriter – in triplicate, of course. One copy would be lodged in the village files and would serve to register the arrangement more-or-less officially. None of this cost a drachma; in England, the solicitor's bill would have been more than the first month's rent. As we drove back to Astratigos, Susan started counting on her fingers. I asked her what she was doing. "Somehow, I've had four glasses of *tschikoudia* already today..." she said. It wasn't yet noon.

We were confident that there would be further negotiations about Antonia's brother's land but we were disappointed in our expectations that the matter would be settled while we were still in Crete. Marianna now held our power-of-attorney and Dimitris, our engineer, had been warned that we might need a speedy survey of the site. There was nothing more we could do but return to Kent and wait.

CHAPTER THIRTEEN

Gypsy Court was ours no longer – subject to contract, of course. While we had been in Crete, the only two people in the universe who wanted a house exactly like the "gypsy cart" had walked into the estate agent's office. One of life's great mysteries had been tested almost to destruction and found to be true: for every seller there's a buyer. All you need is patience! The agent had provisionally arranged for our buyers to see the cottage as soon as we returned. Whatever he had arranged was going to be okay with us if it had the remotest chance of leading to a sale.

Our viewers liked everything we showed them – and they also wanted to move in sooner rather than later because they had sold their own house. We said a little prayer, "Afrata which art in heaven…" Despite the initial flurry of a hurry, in the end it took some months before the deal was completed. The Curse of The Chain was upon us and somewhere back down the line of transactions, of which ours was the last, difficulties between unknown sellers and their buyers blighted everyone's plans. However, we needed the time; we had fallen into the habit of waiting for something – or someone – to turn up and had left many things undone. Our plan had always looked so simple: sell the house, pack the furniture into a container for shipping and make the journey from England to Crete an adventure, driving all the way, taking the pugs with us and camping out each night. As yet, we didn't even have a suitable car or a tent and there were many other matters that we had to attend to.

Books, for example. They turned out to be a chore that was prolonged by my inability to make a decision. I had never been able to discard a book; consequently I had hundreds of musty-smelling titles stacked away that I had acquired, often inexplicably, on my journey through life – which seemed to have taken me via a lot of secondhand shops, jumble sales and, later, boot fairs. While many of my books were undoubtedly still of interest to someone, I didn't think that they were worth the expense of exporting them to Crete. I had a surprisingly large number of titles which time had relegated to the less-than-useful category. I was particularly well-stocked with elderly phrase books in various languages and a lot of books that were downright unreadable either because they were damaged or they were boring. Nevertheless, each one needed close examination before its fate could be decided.

My well-thumbed copy of *Soldier's Speak Easy: French and German for the British Fighting Forces*, inscribed in faded 1940s ink, "This book belongs to Rita Allen", was the first to be tossed into the reject box. I wondered if an Amazonian Rita had ever needed to say, "Help me to dig a trench here. Here is a spade. Can you lend me a pick-axe?" or, probably *hors de combat* at this point, "I have been constipated for several days. Please give me an aperient." I had a number of Greek phrase books that I discarded, feeling certain that, "Can I hire a donkey?" and "What size of plate do you use?" were now redundant in general usage. From other genres in my decrepit collection, *Scouting for Boys*, which hadn't belonged to Rita but whose pages had been vigorously felt-tipped by a boondoggling toddler, *The Compleat Angler* – now incomplete – and a lot of gung-ho adventure books from an inferior sub-species of the *Biggles Pulls it Off* variety were also discarded. I decided that *Facts and Fancies*, which in 1942 forecast that "the experience gained by parachute troops may lead to this becoming a common way of descending from non-stop air liners. The passenger will just be 'dropped off' near his home…" was another one for the bin, despite its excellent condition. The last one out was *Ups and Downs: The Story of a Newspaper Boy*, a saccharine Victorian tract that I had bought because I thought I'd borrow the title for my autobiography. I made up a box of such titles and managed to persuade a secondhand bookseller to swop them for a huge family bible, published in 1877. Although the bible's binding was badly damaged, I thought that Melkhizedek, my monkish friend, might like to have such a volume. The bookseller said it was worth £15 – cash – but because it would be going to a good home he'd agree to an exchange. I carted the weighty volume all the way to Crete only to discover that a sacrilegious vandal had ripped out some interesting pages from the Old Testament. Fortunately, Deuteronomy, chapter XXVIII, verse 27, a favourite of mine, was still intact and I conjured up an image of the bookseller as I read: "The Lord will smite thee with the botch of Egypt, and with the emerods, and with the scab, and with the itch, whereof thou canst not be healed."

Our car was another problem. We were driving a totally unsuitable vehicle for rural Cretan roads: a fast and smooth-running two-litre Citroën ZX saloon. We wanted something more robust, a workhorse that could take the ruts in the road, be repaired with a hammer, tow trailers of grapes and cart a goat to the vet. We wanted something substantial and probably army-surplus. Unfortunately, our ideal vehicle – a Land Rover – was too expensive to buy, run and maintain in our new, penny-conscious world. We found the answer in the used-car columns of the *Exchange & Mart*: a Citroën 2CV, the sturdy little vehicle allegedly originally designed to carry a stout French peasant and his well-fattened pig across ploughed fields to the local abattoir. Our 10-year-old *deux chevaux* was a rather sprauncy-looking black-and-maroon rust-spotted "Charleston Special" with chrome headlamps. It was still a very good-looking car, with one major drawback for anyone driving in the UK – it was of Belgian origin and was left-hand drive. The owner wanted just £250 for it, which included an unopened repair manual. We bought it and drove it straight round to an MoT test centre, where it failed – but only because the nearside rear lamp was brighter than the offside, there was no rear fog warning light, the rear shock absorbers were leaking and the exhaust emissions were too high. Not bad for £250! A 2CV fan later told me that I could have got most of my money back just by selling the chrome headlamps at an enthusiasts' rally. We got the repairs done and spent the time before our departure driving the little car as hard as we could to see if it would break down. It never did – not in England, anyway!

We had decided to go to Crete whether or not we could have the land adjacent to our Afratan plot. Gypsy Court had proved so hard to sell that we weren't going to risk losing our buyers simply because we didn't have another house to go to. If Antonia's brother wouldn't sell us his land, we'd look around elsewhere in Afrata for a bigger plot, using Jakovos's ground-floor flat as a base from which to search. No sooner had we decided this than the telephone rang. God works in a mysterious way... The call was from Athens, offering us the land we wanted at a price we would pay if we had to. As was probably expected of us, we demurred and put forward a counter-offer, which was grudgingly accepted – if we would settle the matter promptly. Susan immediately telephoned both Marianna and Dimitris in Hania and they promised to get to work immediately. She then thought she should telephone Jakovos to check that he was getting on with the building work for which we had given him half-a-year's rent in advance. His reply to our enquiry was predictable: "No problem!"

We had a shopping-list of tasks, which we worked through. The pugs were a major paperwork problem. We only needed our passports but the dogs had to be properly documented for each of the countries that we would pass through on our journey: France, Switzerland, Italy and Greece. The Ministry of Agriculture, Fisheries and Food set out the rules for exporting pugs from England. The dogs, after having been vaccinated against rabies, had to be given a clean bill of health by one of the ministry's local veterinary inspectors – but not more than 48 hours before their departure from England. Our departure would have to be fine-tuned to fit in with the inspector's examination. Eventually, Pug and Mavros were issued with Form 2904EHC for France, which was valid for 10 days, Form 2901EHC for Switzerland, valid for only six days, Form 2903EHC for Italy, valid for a full 30 days, and Form 1530EHC for Greece, valid for 10 days. It was an expensive palaver, which we went through because the dogs were threatened with imprisonment – or worse – if their paperwork wasn't in order. The first thing to be thrown away when we arrived in Afrata was the bulky file of Min of Ag and Fish bumf. We had chunnelled from Dover, motored across Europe and sailed across the Adriatic, but although everyone wanted to pat the pugs not once did anyone seek to check their papers.

The sale of Gypsy Court moved towards its completion and we did all that we could to prepare for the journey ahead. We were keeping most of our furniture, sending it to Crete the long way round on the good ship *Mormed*, which would arrive in Iraklion from Tilbury many days after we had reached Afrata. Our departure for Crete was arranged and we spent the time between leaving Gypsy Court and setting-off towards the Mediterranean staying with our friends Eric and Diana Marsden in their huge Victorian house just beneath the ramparts of Dover Castle. We were on England's doorstep.

It was on Dover beach, listening to the sound of the sea stirring the shingle, that I began to have doubts. Susan didn't have any doubts; she was convinced that we were doing the right thing. I wasn't. Like Matthew Arnold on the same beach, I was swept with "confused alarms of struggle and flight". I agonised. I hadn't wanted to emigrate when I was in my twenties so why should I want to do so in my late forties? I had always thought that people who retired from the places they knew to unfamiliar seaside towns – just to die – were daft. Was this what I was doing? Was a house on a Cretan mountainside overlooking the sea really that different from a bungalow in the back streets of Bognor? I felt "Anglo-Saxon" in my bones and I liked enough of England and things English not to want to flee completely. Slowly, the "confused alarms" quietened down. If I remained in England I would eventually feel it in my Anglo-Saxon bones; I no longer liked the cold and damp winters – or the attendant bills for house-heating. It became clear to me that I had lost sight of one of our main reasons for choosing to live in Crete. Older Cretans, like the 83-year-old Dagounoyianni, enjoy a quality of life unheard of for most elderly inhabitants of northern European countries. They are healthier, they live longer and they still count for something in the sum of things. The young happily talk to the old, and the old delight in the company of the young. Then a visit to my expensive "private" South African émigré dentist reminded me that one of the jewels in the British crown – the NHS – had had a good few carats knocked off it. After he had extracted a couple of thousand pounds, the writing was on the wall: I had to find a way of protecting my savings and making my slender income stretch. Dental treatment was cheaper in Crete, along with nearly everything else. In fact, with an efficient solar heater there were no heating bills for most of the year and Greece hadn't yet got around to local rates, council tax or, heaven help us, a poll tax. I brought my train of thoughts to a halt by reaching for my "lucky" Chinese coin and tossing it: the side with more squiggles would mean "Go!" It came down on the side with fewer squiggles. What does a Chinese coin know anyway? I was going. Life in a Cretan mountain village would be nothing like life in a semi-detached bungalow in Bognor Regis. That much I was sure of. I agreed with King George V – "Bugger Bognor"!

I returned to the house in Dover's Victoria Place to find Eric, a former *Sunday Times* foreign correspondent in Africa and the Middle East, working on his memoirs. Eric had been a journalist all his life and the only differences that retirement brought were that he could no longer claim any expenses and there was no certainty that he would get paid for his writings. When he was a young man, the asthmatic Eric had been told by his doctor that if he wanted to continue breathing he shouldn't stay living and working in Manchester, the newspaper world's second city. This was a long time ago, before the "greening" of Britain's industrial centres occurred, following the dramatic switch from manufacturing things to the buying and selling of houses as the country's main wealth-creating activity. Eric had found work as a journalist in Kenya but his journalistic integrity and inability to temporise got him into serious difficulties with the post-colonial ruling regime. Eric looked up from penning his account of a turbulent life in Nairobi and sighed. "Diana thinks we should go and live in a 'mobile home' in California," he said. Such is life; one day the Foreign Secretary's making a statement about you in the chamber of the House of Commons, the next you're fighting off the threat of a move to a Californian trailer park. If going to Crete was better than becoming a bungalow-dweller on the English Costa Geriatrica, it was infinitely better than living in a caravan – which itself was to be preferred to inhabiting a cardboard shanty cobbled together underneath one of London's many flyovers. My crisis had passed; I would definitely commit myself to living in Crete.

If the 2CV had had gunwales, it would have been packed to them. I had even had to fit a luggage rack to the boot-lid. The day we set off, a rather gloomy Eric came and shook hands. "Keep in touch," he said. I stopped myself from asking: "Here or in California?" Diana, who shared my enthusiasm for junk-collecting, made us a generous farewell present from her Aladdin's cave: two heavily-chromed Art Deco light fittings with six period glass shades. The container had long since gone and I had to find room in the 2CV for these treasures, alongside the pugs' travelling-cage, a tent and all the other things needed for camping-out, suitcases of clothes, an extra spare wheel, a battery and a couple of boxes of things that we had overlooked when leaving Gypsy Court. Packing it all in was one thing, getting it out would be another.

The Dover-Afrata run took us nine days. We went under the English Channel on *Le Shuttle*. There was no danger of seasickness on this antiseptically-clean, smooth and fast route but it denied us the one opportunity that people leaving England really need to have: it's impossible to wave goodbye to England, to watch the White Cliffs of Dover disappear into your past. The pugs were unimpressed, choosing to snooze in their cage on the back seat of the car. We followed their example and stayed in the car. There was nowhere else to go. It was a blandly-efficient but emotionally-blank start to our adventure.

We drove off onto French soil, leaving a trail of oil behind us. The oil-cooler at the front of the engine had sprung a leak. This was definitely a time to shout, *"Merde!"* I found a Citroën garage, where, after a cursory look, the switched-off proprietor dismissively told me that the car was *"kaput"*. I chose to ignore this totally unexpected and unhelpful response and bought five litres of his cheapest engine oil instead. *"Bonne chance,"* he said, with a sneer that made me wish I'd hung on to *Soldier's Speak Easy*, which I was sure would have had an appropriate phrase for the occasion. Possibly something incorporating the words, "smug bastard".

Our plan was to camp out each night, although intermittent rain dampened our initial enthusiasm. The first two French campsites were properly organised, clean *and* well-drained, but the third night we slithered to a halt at a huge site, where we were allocated a numbered pool of mud in which to pitch our tent. When I complained, a horsy young English billeter told me to trot around, find somewhere drier and report back to her – if I succeeded. "We really can't be held responsible for the weather," she declared. We stayed because we had nowhere else to go. The dogs enjoyed it, however, and eight muddy paws scampered excitedly around making a mess inside the two-and-a-half person tent, at the back of which was the half-person compartment separated off from the main section by zippered nylon mesh. This was the dogs' bedroom. The first night it was behind our heads as we slept cheek by jowl with Pug and Mavros; the second night we turned around and stuck our noses close to the tent's open door-flaps. We hadn't allowed for nocturnal flatulence – theirs, not ours. The "whoopee cushions" farted – and snored – all through the night like two beery old men and they turned the tiny tent into a nylon gas-holder. It was a reeking nightmare.

The car was losing oil almost as quickly as I could pour it in, but I felt we could make it to Crete if the problem didn't worsen. Driving in France was a pleasant experience in which the camaraderie of fellow road-users was frequently demonstrated. They would approach me wherever we parked our car and point to the puddle of hot oil which would be forming beneath the engine. I would smile, nod knowingly and from my limited stock of French say, *"Excusez-moi."* This inappropriate response invariably prompted gesticulations intended to convey the seriousness of my situation. All I could do was to shrug my shoulders and contort my face into a half-smile-half-grimace. I thought that my response was rather Gallic, but it usually provoked a contemptuous or despairing: *"Imbécile!"* They were probably right.

We decided to by-pass Switzerland because the trail of engine oil we were leaving everywhere would probably get us arrested and so on the fourth day we drove over the Alps into Italy and began our descent into the motorways from hell. Egomaniac Italian car-drivers and bloody-minded ferry-chasing lorry drivers made no allowance for the heavily-laden old 2CV's limited performance and we were bullied every kilometre of the way by rubber-scorching hustlers who would concede nothing as their vehicles veered and screamed all around us. I wouldn't have been much less in control if I'd driven with my eyes shut. That evening we found a run-down little campsite by a river. The ground was lumpy, the shower block was primitive, we were plagued by mosquitoes, it was hot and the pugs were farting. We decided there and then: no more camping.

The next day, in Ancona, where we had missed the ferry, we strode into a smart travel agency and demanded, tongues-in-cheeks, an inexpensive but comfortable hotel which would accept the pugs and provide overnight garaging for our car. To our amazement they found one for us, although when we drove on to the hotel forecourt, the hotel manager balked at housing our grimy little saloon, which was now leaking oil like a beached tanker. Fortunately, the dogs were very much to his taste, being small and short-haired, and he booked us in. Bliss! We took showers, put on clean clothes, locked the pugs in the lavatory – which we thought was the best place for them – and went out in search of dinner. When we returned, we took the dogs for a walk and then locked them back in the lavatory, hanging the hotel's "Do Not Disturb" sign on the knob to remind us not to open the door too quickly in the morning. We were determined to have a good night's sleep.

The following afternoon we got on the ferry for Greece. Unfortunately, the ferry booking-clerk, who was obviously daft about funny little dogs, had fallen instantly in love with our two. She turned aside our request for on-board kennelling for them and allocated us a spacious air-conditioned "family" cabin so that we could all travel together. This wasn't what we had planned, but we could hardly say no to the roomy accommodation that our four-legged friends' winning ways had got for us. Once again, Pug and Mavros would have to be locked in the lavatory... We all enjoyed the day and a half we spent at sea, although the "whoopee cushions" saw more of the lavatory than they did of the Adriatic. They both had a deep hostility to seagulls, although where this came from was a mystery to us. The sound of a seagull on TV would provoke uncontrollable excitement from them; we feared that they'd leap into the wide blue yonder to reach one in the flesh. We couldn't take the risk of losing them at sea; the lavatory was better for them during the day – and it was definitely the best place for them during the night.

Patras, our destination, came into view in the late evening. We drove down the gangway, on to Greek soil and immediately ground to a halt. The engine had stalled and would not start again. It was the battery, which had not been charging properly. Fortunately, I had another one but never expecting to need it, I had packed it away in the most inaccessible place. While just behind us the giant ferry continued to disgorge its load of container

Pug

lorries, trucks and tourist cars and caravans, we emptied out the car. A port policeman stood idly by watching us. Susan put the pugs on their leads and walked them around. From the stream of passing traffic, I saw someone point from an English car to the armed policeman and then at the pugs. I heard the words,

"Probably sniffer dogs..." The policeman looked at the pugs and then at Susan. "Where do these dogs come from?" he asked. "England," answered Susan, ready to get their papers from the car. "They look Chinese to me," he said suspiciously. "No, I assure you that they're English. I'll show you their papers," offered Susan. "Papers? What papers?" queried the policeman. "I was only asking..." The new battery worked and we were on our way again, but we had lost a valuable hour.

The next ferry we needed was departing from Gythio, in the southern Peloponnese. We had about eight hours to cover a couple of hundred miles of unknown, tortuous and mostly mountainous coastal road – in the dark. As we were going up our first mountain, we had our second technical hitch: the fan belt snapped.

By the time I had fitted a new one, we had to forego any snacking or catnapping and drive through the night. It was madness to race relentlessly along this road but the ferry only sailed twice-weekly and we didn't want to kick our heels in Gythio because of a near miss. We didn't quite make it for the official checking-in time but we could see the small ferry still being loaded. We drew up on the quayside and joined the short queue of vehicles, edging slowly forward until we drew level with the ferry master – who then officiously decided not to allow us aboard. Susan went into Greek fishwife-mode and I flailed my arms in support. After a ferocious argy-bargy between the three of us – with the pugs barking support from their cage in the car – the ferry master gave in and we rolled into the car-hold for the last stage of our journey.

The ferry meandered from Gythio to the islands of Kithira and Antikithira, before steaming slowly on to Kastelli. We were desperately hungry and thirsty, having had nothing to eat or drink for hours. The aged ship was Spartan, the few deckchairs had to be reserved by sitting on them, and there was only one item of food on the menu. The four of us sat on the deck with a luncheon meat sandwich each. We struck a deal with Pug and Mavros; they had our meat and we had their bread. We were all unsatisfied. The only reward from this interminable voyage was the gradual appearance of scruffy old Kastelli, which sat, like a scatter of confetti at the edge of the Bay of Kissamos. The choppy waters of the bay stretched between the two fingers of Crete's westernmost peninsulas. To port were the cloud-hugged, pinkish slopes of the Rodopou peninsula, on which Afrata nestled, while to starboard, we closely followed the much-smaller Gramvousa peninsula's coastline of steep and barren cliffs broken occasionally by rocky slopes peppered with scrubby greenery.

Our arrival was as anti-climactic as our departure. We were on an internal Greek ferry and so no one was around to check anything. We just drove out of the harbour and turned left in the direction of Kastelli proper. We had done it; we were now in Crete. We had been on the road for eight nights and although the dipstick had been in and out of the engine, like a thermometer checking the progress of a sick patient's fever, the 2CV had not let us down. It had, however, used 20 litres of oil and was now haemorrhaging badly.

The Stork was not far away and we resolved to stop and eat. Dimitris welcomed us, admired the car but expressed some doubts about the pugs. "Do they bite?" he asked. "No," I said. "They just fart a lot…" He backed off at the sound of this and disappeared to fetch our order. We were definitely back in Crete – the wine was free.

CHAPTER FOURTEEN

We arrived in Afrata to a greeting that made us feel that we'd come home. Unfortunately, "home" didn't turn out to be quite what we had expected. Jakovos's wife informed us that "some superficial details" remained to be sorted out in our flat but, otherwise, it was ready for us. Maybe our northern European attitudes were too deeply ingrained but somehow we couldn't see the absence of a kitchen sink, kitchen cupboards, bathroom taps and internal doors as merely "superficial". We also thought that a WC without water was a serious matter requiring immediate attention. Furthermore, the flat was on a very public ground floor alongside the village square and we thought that the shutters should have been fitted before our arrival. Jakovos returned from work to find us in need of consolation. "No problem!" was, as ever, his response to our complaints. He proposed that we trotted around the corner to use the *kafeneon's* outside lavatory until he got things sorted out. "When will that be?" I asked. "Oh, tomorrow – or the day after..." he replied. In Crete, this promise should never be taken as anything more than a tentative nod in the direction of the future. "Tomorrow", in Greek, has the same loaded meaning as *"manyana"* – but without the Spanish sense of urgency! We never did get a door on the lavatory, external shutters or a promised independent water-heater but the other "superficial matters" were more-or-less sorted out – within a fortnight.

Our furniture wasn't due for another week, during which time we had only the things that were in the 2CV, the back seat of which I removed so that we could enjoy sitting on a "sofa". Our camp beds were very uncomfortable and Georgia, Kostis's wife, offered us the loan of two single beds. The "mattresses" turned out to be the two halves of a sprung double mattress that had been sawn straight down the middle! The first night we each tried to sleep at attention, afraid even to turn over in case one of the severed springs ripped open an artery or whipped out an eyeball. There was no resident doctor in Afrata, the one in Kolymbari was usually a beginner posted in to get some hands-on experience – and the hospital casualty department was on the other side of Hania. The second night we resurrected the narrow, folding beds from our camping expedition, thinking it was better to be stiff than sorry. Kostis, who had seen the two old deckchairs we had just found for ourselves at the local rubbish tip, called and asked if we would like a table. It was circular with a plastic top mounted on well-rusted steel legs. It had been left out in the sun and the rain for a long time and the plastic top had curled up like a hat-brim, away from the swollen chipboard base. When we ate at it, it was like eating in the Red Sea between the two waves parted by Moses. It wasn't possible for four people to use the table. We were living like a couple of tramps squatting in an empty building and surrounded by the discarded odds and ends of better-off folk.

For more than a week our kind neighbours looked after us until the removal van arrived. Breakfast was particularly memorable in those first few days. Georgia insisted on making it for us every morning. We would have settled for coffee but she wouldn't hear of it. No, every morning there it was: steaming bowls of freshly-boiled goat's milk. I thought of England and creamy, cold, cow's milk fresh from the fridge poured over crispy cornflakes. I started by hating hot milk but by the end of the week, obviously becoming acclimatised, I merely disliked it. Nevertheless, it wasn't possible to say "no thank you" to Georgia. Petrula brought around dinner-plates of barbecued meat or fish and Dimitra gave us a pile of one of her robust Cretan specialities: courgette flower heads and sweet peppers stuffed solid with savoury rice. Aristides and Irini had us around to eat and we also went upstairs to dine with our landlord and landlady. This was an exercise in diplomacy because we felt aggrieved that their promises had not been kept. The situation worsened, with the weather, as the weeks slipped by into early winter. Our flat seemed to be last in line for any hot water produced by the inadequate rooftop solar heater, unless we got up before anyone else and siphoned it off. A villager overheard us complaining about the discomfort of starting the day with a cold shower. "What do you want a wash in the morning for?" he asked. Village life had revealed itself!

The day that our furniture arrived was a village event. The huge container truck could be heard struggling up the mountain road and everyone rushed out, with kids shouting, "It's coming, it's coming!" It was as if a circus had come to Afrata. Kyriacos brought an easy chair to our front door so that he could sit and watch the proceedings in comfort. The Bulgarian delivery workers employed by the Greek contractor sweated to haul stuff from the oven-like inside of the deep container and every few minutes they would plaintively call out for water. Villagers helped speed up the unloading by carrying in boxes and furniture. Eventually, the truck drove off and we discovered that we could hardly get into our flat. Kostis said we could put some of our stuff in the *kafeneon* and Yiannis offered us one of his outside sheds. As for the rest, it would be like living in the 2CV – everything would have to be cunningly packed in.

Slowly, we settled into a routine, but before we could get too involved in home-making we had to get the car sorted out. Here we were lucky: one of Hania's Citroën specialists was a son of the village and when he discovered that we were sort-of fellow Afratans, he set to work with a will and declared that repairing the car was, "No problem..." It was a problem, but only because spare parts often have to be sent to Crete by ferry from stockpiles in Athens. This is a process that sometimes works well and sometimes doesn't. Our bits were delayed but we continued to drive around, topping up the oil on a twice-daily basis. The car was also a problem with its GB sticker and English number plates. According to the British Consulate in Iraklion we would only be allowed to drive the car for six months and then it would have to be taken out of the country or taken off the road – unless we paid to have it re-registered with Greek number plates. We went to the local customs office in Hania to find out how much this would cost.

"Don't ask! You wouldn't want to know!" said the first official we spoke to in the harbour-front customs house. We persisted and grudgingly he took us to another office and explained our problem to a superior, who looked up at us for just long enough to say,

"Throw the car away!" Susan insisted that we really did want to know. The two officials looked at each other, shrugged and then shouted out for colleagues to join them. Three more officials came into the room. There was a lot of jabbered conversation, consultation of charts and stabbing at a desktop calculator. The superior official then sat back, folded his arms and with an I-told-you-so smirk gave us a figure in French francs. We calculated what it would be in pounds sterling. "£3,500!" I exclaimed. "That's impossible!" added Susan. "That's what it is," said the superior official. And that's what it was, although, of course, we never paid it. Much as we had grown fond of our 2CV, we were not going to shell out 14 times what it had cost us just for two stamped-out bits of Greek tinplate. It sounded like good old-fashioned banditry to me and a very long way from the community spirit that was supposed to harmonise dealings in the new Europe. Numerous victims of this bureaucratic brigandry had complained to Brussels but the Greek authorities had a bold and pat answer: the money wasn't an import duty – perish the thought! – it was a "special tax". If our 2CV had been Greek, we could have re-registered it in the UK for 14 times *less* than we had paid for it.

Antonia's brother's land was his no longer and our architect was working on the plans for a new house on our enlarged site. He had our "roughs" to guide him and he knew that we wanted, among other things, four terraces for sitting outside at different times of the day, a covered area for shelter from the rain, a large basement, two bathrooms and a very large living room. While he was at work we explored our new surroundings and discovered more about our neighbourhood and its inhabitants.

Afrata is a village of about 150 souls – most of them Greek Orthodox – and gradually we met nearly all of them. At the *kafenea* we also often fell into conversation with visitors who were as interesting as the permanent residents. There were very few villagers that we didn't speak to at some time or other. Among those we met and got to know in our early days in the village was Themistocles Tzanakis, the "Bird Man of Afrata". He was a rare find in Greece – a genuine animal lover. He had a huge number of birds, from strutting turkeys to homing pigeons, living around his house and because he was reluctant to slaughter any of them, his flock proliferated and he could often be seen, like a latter-day St Francis, talking to them. His favourite was a superannuated chicken that he had wrenched to safety from the jaws of a vicious rat and whose terrible wounds he had stitched together with household needle-and-thread. The bird, much-scarred, survived its ordeal and was obviously devoted to Themis, his saviour.

We hadn't yet been in every house in Afrata, but we suspected that Themis was probably the only villager with his own cocktail bar. It was a DIY-construction of a high wood-and-stone bar with long-legged stools for the drinkers. A large wine barrel sat in one corner, a small one – of *tschikoudia* – was perched on the bar and birdcages hung from the walls. This was definitely a "free" house; the bar was solely for entertaining callers. Themis invited me in to admire it. "Do you know what it needs, Antoni?" he asked as he poured us two *tschikoudias*. Apart from a 1960s lava lamp, I couldn't think. Themis supplied the answer: "A woman, Antoni!" He knew exactly what he wanted: a naked one – with large breasts and long blonde hair. "You are an artist! Make me one for the back of my bar!" he said, pointing at a blank alcove. "Well, I don't know. I suppose I could paint a bird in there," I said, thinking that that might satisfy his demands and get me off the hook. "Ah! You understand exactly what I want!" he declared, clapping me on the back enthusiastically. In his earlier years, Themis had spent some time in Liverpool and had a good grasp of English slang. He was very disappointed when he discovered that what I had in mind was a parrot or a toucan.

Then there was Nick, who had been educated in Wales, and who ran the program for the young Americans who came to Grimviliana. I encountered him at the Kali Kardia, sitting with a group of locals eating the head of something, sheep or goat probably, but I wouldn't like to say. I was invited to join in, and an as yet-unknown villager cut a singed ear off the head and urged me to eat it. Encouraged by Nick, I did. It was a somewhat disappointing gastronomic experience: it was exactly like chewing a singed ear! Nick then produced a macho hunting knife and winkled the eyes out of the skull, proclaiming them to be "ambrosia", the food that had conferred everlasting youth and beauty on the gods. I declined to partake, but another – classically inclined and obviously hopeful – guest at this impromptu feast picked up the still-slimy balls and juggled with them before popping one into his mouth. Strangely, his snaffling of this ocular snack went unchallenged. He played with the eye, as if it were a gob-stopper, rolling it from side-to-side for nearly a minute before surreptitiously spitting it out. I was curious because I had always thought that the eyes were a rare and much-sought-after delicacy. I wrapped up the unsucked eye in a paper napkin and took it home to feed to one of the pugs. It was Mavros who grabbed it. He wolfed it down in a single gulp, but then he never chews anything except table-legs. When I took him for his walk the next morning the poor little chap's own eyeballs bulged from his head as he crouched and strained. I took a discrete look at his rear – out of which popped the previous day's eye, intact!

Our new neighbours would often still give us things. Almonds, for example. Everybody in Afrata had almond trees; we even had a couple ourselves but this fact seemed to have gone unnoticed and we were presented with bag after bag. The nuts were so cheap in the market that we couldn't see the point of hours of mindless labour cracking them open, but this was definitely a minority view. All over the village, men and women, old and not-so-old, sat on their doorsteps cracking nuts. Some used a favourite stone, others a little hammer. Georgia cracked hers on the cement terrace of the Kali Kardia using a solid brass weight from the antique set of scales she kept at the back of the *kafeneon*. A tourist was watching her one day and gestured a request to be allowed to take her photograph. She didn't mind at all. "It's a timeless sight," waxed the tourist, who had imbibed a tad too much of Kostis's lunchtime wine and was now full of the romance and the uninterrupted continuity of life in rural Crete. "She will have been cracking nuts in that way for hundreds of years," he trilled. I told him that it was a good thing Georgia didn't speak English – she was only 50!

We also met Papa Antonis, the local Greek orthodox priest, who looked positively cherubic and whose easy-going, friendly manner made him popular with everyone in the village. Then there was Roxanne, the voluble keeper of the Afratan taverna which claimed François Mitterand as one of its patrons. Mitterand, when President of France, had taken time off from a conference being held in Kolymbari to visit Roxanne's and partake of her rabbit *stifado*. This partaking boosted trade at the taverna and established Roxanne's status as a local celebrity – much to the chagrin of Afrata's other *"cordons bleus"*. Personally, I think they fry eggs rather well in Afrata...

It became very clear that we had deluded ourselves in assuming that there were few foreigners living in these parts. There were lots, tucked away in the small villages that dot western Crete. The Cypriot-born sexagesimal Nick, who was actually British although thought of by many as American, and his wife, who was an American, were just two of many. There was, for example, Wilf, an Englishman living quietly, as everyone appeared to, in Astratigos with his wife, Pam. He had a peculiar problem – the Greeks found it all but impossible to say "Wilf" and so they called him "Petros"! His near-neighbour was Patrick Leung. Dieter came to Afrata from Germany via Israel. We met an Englishwoman living half-a-dozen villages away who said that she had lectured at the London college from which I had retired. Ian, who I met at a Greek language school in Hania, told me that he'd come across a Glaswegian couple, an American bricklayer, a German psychiatrist, an Italian doctor and an Englishman in a remote village who worked for Sotheby's.

I lost track of the number of incomers we encountered who claimed to be either "artists" or "writers". Hardly anyone seemed to want to own up to being a redundant invoice clerk or a retired teacher or something similarly unsexy. I remembered an unsuccessful painter-friend in England who used to tell people that he was a "government artist" – he meant that he was good at drawing the dole! It sometimes seemed that nobody was retired – hurt, early or otherwise – or unemployed, except for me. Susan claimed that I was unusual in owning up to Early Retirement. I pointed out that although early-retired I did at least have some small claims to an identity as an artist. After all, Sir Roger de Grey, the late President of the Royal Academy, had once patted my shoulder and told me: "Your work is very nearly very good." I think it was a compliment.

It was in Afrata that I think I received another compliment. We had been invited to dinner at Nick's house, where we met a visiting American writer, Robert Fulghum. I told him some of my stories of everyday life in the village. In return, he chortled and told me that he thought they were at least as good as some of the tales he'd read in books of a similar vein. It sounded like a compliment! In any event, I decided to accept his encouraging suggestion that I should write a book... Other passers-by at this time included Melvyn, an English cyclamen buff who spent his holidays tracking down unusual plants, and Jesper, a Danish sexologist, who claimed to have a professional interest in "the Cretan experience of orgasm". We wished him luck; it seemed like a line of inquiry fraught with the potential for a fatal misunderstanding. We also met Gertie, a passionately spiritual German artist who had fallen in love with the atmosphere of the Rotonda, where our friend Melkhizedek was the incumbent.

Despite all these new faces, we were definitely living a different life in Afrata from the one we had had in England. One evening, Susan returned from walking the dogs... "Themis is watching TV," she reported. "Which channel?" I enquired. "I don't know," she sighed. "Doesn't he watch TV most evenings?" I asked. "I suppose so," she said resignedly. Yes, life had changed. We were having difficulties adjusting to our new regime, although "regime" suggested a discipline and structure that our daily round no longer had. We weren't lonely and we certainly weren't bored but we still had to come to terms with our new life, the style of which posed some challenges. Susan, for example, didn't actually miss going to work but she felt the absence of the intellectual challenge that daily computer problem-solving had offered her. I was better off because I had spent most of my working life thinking about retirement and too many intellectual challenges gave me a headache. The only thing that I really missed by not being at work

– apart from the money – was the exhilarating sense of freedom that used to flood over me when I accelerated out of the employees' car park. Now we were both "free" all day, every day – and while I revelled in the fact, it was going to take the industrious Susan some time to get used to the fact. The truth is that after a lifetime of wage-earning labour, most people have to work even harder to reinvent themselves as lotus-eaters. Voltaire pointed out the problem when he said, in *Candide*, that "man was born to suffer from the restlessness of anxiety or from the lethargy of boredom". Between these high and low roads there is an unmapped middle way that is the route to contentment. Finding it's the only problem!

We were also having a little local difficulty because we were now together all of the time and minor irritations, which hadn't been mentioned before, were in danger of erupting into major rows. Susan revealed that she was exasperated by my habit of squeezing the middle of the tube of toothpaste. I told her that that was nothing compared to how I felt about her inability to leave a pen beside the telephone. We consoled ourselves with the thought that we were living under difficult conditions in which we could do little except wait for the building work to start on our new house. That seemed a long way off because, although we had approved the architect's plans for a large, three-bedroomed, island-style house, there was still an enormous amount of paperwork to be done before we could even apply for our building permit.

It was now late summer but that didn't mean a thing here in terms of weather: it was fine every day. We felt that it was time to take a break from our rather bare routine in Afrata. We decided to take the *Gramvousa Express*, a large pleasure-boat that sailed every day from Kastelli's harbour for a long day-trip to uninhabited Gramvousa, the flat-topped triangular islet that we had seen from the ferryboat carrying us on the last stage of our journey from England. The boat ride took us northwards back past the familiar but forbidding rocky grey cliffs that plunged vertically into the sea. We seemed to be the only people enjoying the fresh sea air; everyone else on deck was smoking. The ship's loudspeaker gave out its messages in Greek, German, Italian, Danish – and English, although there weren't many of *us* on board. At the base of the passing cliffs could be seen a distinctive bathtub "tide mark" which showed how much western Crete had so far risen from the virtually tide-less sea. Geologically, we had chosen the right part of the island in which to settle; while the west was rising, eastern Crete was actually sinking. Further down the coastline, a huge cave appeared high up in the cliff. Trippers with cameras threw their cigarettes into the wind and rushed to photograph it. While the ship's loudspeaker boomed out that it was the entrance to the ancient city of Agnion, there were squeals from people on the starboard side as discarded burning cigarette-butts rained down on them.

About an hour from Kastelli harbour, the boat turned to port, rounded a headland, and berthed at Gramvousa's small jetty, passing the rusting wreck of an ancient tramp steamer on the way. Some 137 metres above the jetty, the massive 278 meter-long walls of the fortress – built by the Venetians in 1579 and occupied by them until 1692, when it fell to the Ottoman Turks – towered over the boatload of pleasure-seekers. It was a dramatic sight but it failed to attract about a third of the passengers, who made straight for a swim from the sandy bay alongside the jetty. The rest of us climbed the long, steep and rugged footpath to the entrance of the fortress, where a notice warned that overnight camping and other – unspecified – activities were forbidden. A visitor with the look of experience had found something on the ground and a small group of young travellers hungry to hear a tale and have one to tell gathered around him. "Opium pipe…" said the man knowingly, while holding up his find for all to see. Maybe that was the sort of thing the sign was referring to!

The fortress was a picturesque ruin offering splendid views, but it was fraught with danger. English Heritage would never have allowed the public on to the site. There were no proper footpaths and there were lots of unguarded holes down which one could easily fall into deep underground chambers. The thought alone was frightening. As usual in such places in Greece, there were no signs to help visitors understand what they were looking at. Neither were there any lavatories and as a consequence screwed-up bits of tissue paper were to be found behind every bush and pile of old stones.

After a treacherous descent back down the slippery stone-strewn track, half the fortress-trippers went for a cold beer on the boat while the other half opted for the clear waters of the sandy bay. After a while, the boat sounded its horn for the planned departure to the nearby Balos lagoon, where Charles and Diana had taken a honeymoon dip from the royal yacht, *Britannia*. It took only a few minutes to cross from Gramvousa to the lagoon, above which towered a snow-less Matterhorn. Because of the shallows, the captain of the pleasure boat couldn't get in close enough for people to disembark. He offered a choice: get into a flat-bottomed boat that was standing by to ferry visitors ashore – or swim. There were about 120 people on board; six chose to swim. The first swimmer to land turned out to be an Englishwoman from Market Harborough. Her name was Kathy and with her husband, Merv, she was enjoying an energetic holiday. The day before they had trekked the rugged 18-kilometre route of the longest gorge in Europe, the Samaria, in south-western Crete. The four of us sat together on the lagoon's sandy beach. The sea around was a brilliant turquoise-blue, although within the lagoon the stirred-up sand muddied the otherwise clear water. Merv, an irreverent and jocular Scot, waded out into it for a swim, shouting something unintelligible about "the royal *we*."

Around us in the exotic-looking location topless young women either frolicked in the warm water or struck pin-up poses for camera-toting boyfriends. We did a bit of frolicking ourselves before drying off to explore the fringes of the lagoon. It was a mistake to do so. The magic went as we found pile after pile of picnickers' rubbish and those tell-tale scrunched-up tissues. But far worse than that, most of the rockier parts of the beach area were besmirched with black dollops of crude oil, like so many horse-droppings. It was sad to see. We returned to the boat for the journey back to Kastelli. It was an uneventful ride, except for the amusement of watching the mounting frustration of mobile 'phone-users unable to get through to dry land from the now-rolling boat. Watching them took my mind off feeling seasick.

Back in Afrata, the summer days passed into autumn, but with each one we learned more about the villagers, their way of life and their attitudes. It was a shock to discover how prejudiced many of them were. Lots of them instinctively disliked lots of things, from other people's untried cooking to people they had never met. For historical and political reasons they professed a deep hatred of the Turks who, they thought, would return to Crete to lord it over them with despotic cruelty, given half-a-chance. They took every opportunity to disparage the Turks. One elderly woman sincerely believed that her grandfather had seen a Turk playing with a string of worry-beads made from women's nipples. I could easily have got her to believe that my great-grandfather had once seen a Turk in Skegness with worry-beads made from Christian choirboys' testicles! The ancient Greek hostility towards the Turks showed little sign of abating in western Crete.

Not quite as bad as Turks, in Cretan eyes, are the Albanians. There are a lot of them in western Crete, many of them illegal immigrants. From early-morning they hang dejectedly around the main thoroughfares of Hania, Kastelli and the larger villages hoping to be hired for a day's manual work at low pay. They work mainly as unskilled labourers in the fields or on building sites and are popularly believed to be bad in every respect. They have become Greece's favourite whipping boys and they are the subjects of numerous quickfire jokes, which would be frowned upon – if not declared illegal – in more politically correct societies.

There was a sizeable and long-established Jewish community in Hania, but that was before the Germans arrived. One day the city's Jews were rounded up – by ordinary German soldiers; there were never any SS troops on Crete – and loaded on to a boat for the first stage of the journey to the gas-chambers of Auschwitz. These little-known victims of the Holocaust never even made it across the Mediterranean; their vessel went down on the night of the 5th June 1944, midway between Crete and Piraeus. The Germans claimed that it had been torpedoed by a British submarine but, according to Dimitris Kartakis, a doctor in Hania and a writer on that period of Cretan history, the general belief was that the Germans scuppered the boat to rid themselves of the unfortunate Jews as speedily as possible. This tragic tale has little effect on the prejudices of older villagers, among some of whom there are still inexplicably strong anti-Semitic feelings based on nothing except ridiculous stories like the one another old woman from Afrata told me. According to her, when a Jew died the corpse was taken to the synagogue, seated in a special "throne" and a hard-boiled egg placed in each hand. The rabbi and leading members of the congregation then put their hands pat-a-cake fashion on the dead one's head and pressed down hard. If the corpse broke wind that was a sign that it's soul had gone to heaven! When I dismissed the story as nonsense, she insisted, "No! I tell you it's true. A Jew told me himself that this is what happens!"

CHAPTER FIFTEEN

Autumn had arrived and with it, carpets of pink cyclamen. Even layers of "builders'compost" couldn't stop these pretty little wild blooms from breaking through. It was also wine-making time. Once again we trod grapes with the Dagounakis and Platsakis families. Since arriving in Afrata we had not bought any wine; we had only to ask and someone would draw us a bottle-full from his barrel. Even Kostis, whose business it was to sell drink, never charged us for the many bottles we had from him. In Afrata, a bottle of wine always meant a one-and-a-half litre plastic Coca-Cola bottle filled to the brim. The only corks to be seen were the bungs in the top of the barrels. After the grapes had been trodden, and the resulting liquid must poured into the waiting barrels, the village seethed with the sound of fizzing grape-skins wrapped in plastic sacks and packed into old oil-drums. A few weeks later, most of these plastic sacks would be taken to Elias, who ran the village's licensed still, the *kazani*, to be turned into *tschikoudia*. He distilled these leftovers from wine-pressing into the colourless but throat-scorching "Cretan whisky" and took payment in kind, which he would subsequently sell – there being far too much for him to drink. Elias sold us his own-brand spirit at 1,000 drachmas a litre, which compared very well with the price of a bottle of something similar – at least in its effect – from Sainsbury's. Down in Kolymbari there were two *kazania* that would be similarly busy. In Astratigos, there was yet another.

We were not going to have any problem deciding what to drink with our first Cretan Christmas dinner, which was now less than a week away. Our palates had grown to like the local wine and that, with a *tschikoudia* chaser, would satisfy us. The Christmas bird was more of a problem. Setting aside the possibility of further linguistic confusion, Susan was reluctant to ask Themis, who had the finest fowl in the village, for a bird. She had her eye on one of his magnificent free-range turkeys. "He'd probably agree to sell one if we were going to have it as a pet!" she said. We later discovered that Themis didn't mind other people eating his birds –

but he preferred it if they also dispatched them. It was Georgia who solved the poultry problem for us. Although her son, Jakovos, had installed an ostentatious doorbell, she, in common with all our other Cretan callers, preferred to stand outside and shout our names – loudly. When Susan opened the front door, Georgia was standing there in a red pinny and black rubber boots. Only the white cotton-wool beard was missing! "Would you like a chicken for Christmas, Susannah?" she asked. "Oh! Thank you. We would!" answered an unsuspecting Susan. Georgia handed over a black plastic dustbin bag. It was moving. Susan looked inside – and was horrified to see a live chicken flapping about. She turned to me. "Now what do I do?" she asked. We preferred the butcher's chickens, which came dead and oven-ish ready once you'd cut off the claws and a few other bits The sensitive Georgia guessed Susan's problem and promptly offered to wring the poor bird's neck for her. People are very kind here, there's no doubt about it!

Crete was virtually untouched by the commercialisation of Christmas. Constant reminders of it didn't start appearing from early November and the shops were mercifully free˙of syrupy dreams of a white one. The emotional blackmailers who forced the British public to keep the high-street tills ringing were ineffective manipulators here. New Year's eve is a time for celebration, here as everywhere, and it's also when St Basil brings children a present or two, but it's Easter that's the great Greek eating and drinking marathon. Christmas Day seemed just like any other Sunday in the village although for us it didn't turn out quite as expected. Susan had got our Christmas dinner under way and while it was cooking we set off to wish our neighbours the compliments of the season, English-style. We arrived in Dimitra's kitchen to find a white cloth on the table; she had obviously cooked something special. Yiannis came in and we all exchanged Christmas handshakes and hugs. "Sit down," ordered Dimitra, waving at the table, which was set for four. "I've cooked a chicken for us," she said. "Us?" queried Susan. "You're having lunch with us, aren't you?" she queried. Apparently the invitation had been made telepathically but we must have been switched off at the time of transmission. Susan looked me; I shrugged back.

"Of course we are," said Susan brightly. It was only 11 o'clock and if we didn't eat too much we'd be ready for our own chicken at one. On the way back down the hill, we had a *tschikoudia* with Themis and another with Kostis and then we called in on Kyriacos and Petrula, who had their children, grandchildren and great-grandchildren with them. "Ah! There you are!" said Petrula, the cheerful matriarch. "The food's ready..." We got home just in time to save our chicken from disintegration. "I don't suppose you're hungry?" asked Susan. "Only for a rest from eating," I replied. We saved our chicken and had it cold with chips the next day, breaking open a jar of Crosse & Blackwell's Branston pickle that we had brought from England expressly for the purpose.

Yiannis and Dimitra actually issued a formal invitation to us to eat with them on New Year's Eve. We were asked to come at six o'clock – because they liked to get to bed early! We had eaten boiled mutton, the household's favourite dish, and while I sat unpacking bits of it from between my teeth, the old couple entertained us with their reminiscences. If this had been TV's *Mastermind*, Yiannis could have swept the board with his detailed knowledge of "Life in Afrata and Kolymbari 1926-1939", while Dimitra was also pretty good on the subject of nearby Gerani, her home village, which, she recalled, had been a wonderfully shady place until fuel-gathering German soldiers chopped down most of the old trees.

Today, Afratans do their shopping in Kolymbari, Kastelli or Hania, although the greengrocer, the fishmonger and the baker regularly drive up to the village. Afrata also receives visits from itinerant traders who bring lorry-loads of cheap plastic goods and clothing to sell. In the summer, these mobile "barrow-boys" talk unsuspecting villagers into buying brightly coloured garden chairs. Although these chairs have four legs when purchased, one or more often falls off within a few weeks. The village always has at least one three-legged plastic chair awaiting collection by the municipal rubbish cart. The irresistible salesmanship of these cheapjacks also explained the incongruous and frequent sight of aged villagers sporting outlandish Taiwanese sweatshirts – and matching baseball caps – bearing slogans like, "Go for it!"

Yiannis could remember the days before the hawkers could get up to Afrata. The road from Kolymbari wasn't built until 1954 and before that one could get to and from the village only on foot or by donkey, following a steep and narrow track. Once in Kolymbari, there were two small privately-owned buses plying the route to Hania. Dimitra recalled that passengers carrying farm produce for sale were likely to be stopped on the outskirts of Hania and forced to pay a tax. She also remembered that just after the road was built, someone with a lorry started a literally "under-cover" bus service to Hania. The passengers got in the back and were then hidden under a tarpaulin for the run into the city! "Of course," said Yiannis, "the new road stopped short of the village. We had to wait years for it to be continued into the centre of the village and then down to Lower Afrata – and the asphalting didn't come until after that!"

Yiannis could travel up and down the streets of old Kolymbari in his mind's eye and tell you anything you might want to know. The present-day Diktyna fish-taverna had been a bakery and opposite, where there is still a baker's shop, there had been a combined baker's-and-butcher's shop. The old building next to the Diktyna had been the police station – and was used as a jail by the Germans during the war. The smart, modern café standing on its own on the harbour front had been Kolymbari's main olive mill. The old shepherd could remember it all. "And Afrata," he said, "boasted three grocery stores of its own, two of them combined with *kafenea*." One of them was the Asteri, now minus its shop. There was also a saddle-maker, but villagers had to go to Spilia, just south of Kolymbari, to have a horse shod. "The blacksmith is still there," Yiannis chuckled.

"There was no mains water up here in Afrata until 1973," continued Yiannis. "There was a public well, but this didn't produce enough so private ones were dug. My mother once went to draw water from one of these private wells and the owner stopped her and sent her packing. After that, my father built our own family well, on the outskirts of the village. It was six metres in diameter – and it still works," he said. The water was collected in big containers made from skin and carried home by donkey, but if the donkey was busy elsewhere the women of the family would collect the water in *stamnas* – heavy, round-bottomed, two-handled clay jars holding about 10 litres and carried on the shoulders. "I remember going to the well for eight *stamnas* just before I went into labour!" recalled Dimitra, who had had five children.

It was now just before 8 o'clock – four hours to go before St Basil started his rounds. Dimitra yawned and begged us to excuse them. It was their bedtime. Dimitra, however, would get up again at five-to-midnight because she didn't like to miss seeing-in the New Year.

There was a noisy crowd in the Kali Kardia but we were happy enough with our own company – and that of Pug and Mavros, of course. We went home and sat and enjoyed our own reminiscences, like the New Year's Eve in Athens when we had hailed a taxi... Unfortunately, we weren't the only paying passengers and by the time the others had been dropped off, midnight struck with us still a mile from our destination. The taxi-driver was obviously determined to greet the New Year Greek-style. While speeding down a long avenue he turned around, flashed each of us a wide smile, pumped our hands and wished us *"chronia polla!"* – a happy new year. He then produced a firework from the glove compartment in front of him, clenched it in his teeth, lit the fuse with the dashboard cigarette lighter, and counted to ten before hurling it out of the window where it exploded right by our heads like a bazooka rocket!

We would have had our building permit in December, but for the hiatus of Christmas and the New Year, which had brought the slow-grinding cogs of the planning machine to a complete halt. The precious, but often ignored, document arrived in the second week of January. The first people to hear our good news were Manolis Marnerakis, a retired fisherman, and his wife Niki. They invited us into their little old house in upper Afrata to celebrate with a bowl of fish soup – which, to me, looked as if it had been dredged up from the ocean-bed. My favourite soup was a consommé; Cretan fish soup is a lumpy pottage from which cod eyes balefully stare at you. I didn't like the look of it but our hosts urged me to eat. It was delicious. I made a rather belated New Year resolution: to stop being a fussy eater.

The next day we went into Hania for a meeting with our civil engineer. Susan was going to be clerk-of-works for the construction of the house but she confessed to needing someone to hold her hand. Dimitris said he would be pleased to help whenever advice was needed. If we didn't supervise the work ourselves, we'd have to pay Dimitris – and we couldn't afford to have him visit the site every day, although he would be making regular inspections as part of our contract with him. Two Athenian friends from Susan's past had shared their salutary experiences of house-building with us and their advice was to be on site every day when the builders were around, to keep an eye on the work, and when they weren't, in order to watch out for pilferers. We were obviously in for a busy few months, but the work couldn't be started yet because we were in the depths of the Cretan winter. For us, with clear memories of English winters, they were very shallow depths!

Dimitris set out a list of tasks for Susan, whose command of Greek made her the natural choice as overseer. She would have to engage the workforce and bring them in as and when they were required. She would also have to buy all the materials and arrange for their delivery to the site. It sounded quite simple really. Unfortunately, there was also the paperwork. First, she would have to see that the builders stuck to the construction plans and, secondly, she would have to keep proper records in order to get a final rubber stamp of approval for a permanent electricity supply. Then there were the IKA – social security – payments that would have to be calculated and made for all the workers she engaged. Susan's enthusiasm for the task was diminishing. I said I would help.

The list of tasks set out the order in which craftsmen would have to be engaged. First, we needed an excavator to demolish the old stable, which couldn't be incorporated into a new building, and to prepare the site. In the first week of March, we employed a man with a JCB and just as he was about to bring down the stable, Themis suddenly appeared and shouted something that sounded like, "Wait!" but it might have been, "Shit!" Everything stopped. "What is it?" I asked. "Save the floor!" he called out. I remembered that Yiannis had once looked at the floor with more than passing interest. It couldn't be an ancient mosaic or anything like that because the archaeologists had inspected the site before the building permit was granted. It was *kopria* – dung. We had 40 years of compacted mule and goat droppings in that shack. "Excellent stuff," enthused Themis, as he crumbled a lump through his fingers. I salvaged a couple of wheelbarrow-loads and it proved itself to be a potent organic fertiliser. It wasn't enough, however, to compensate for what turned out to be a disastrous start to the building programme. We had estimated 3-4 days of work; it took 13 days. The underlying rock was so hard that the JCB operator could only chip away at it slowly. We had lost nearly two working weeks and our budget was blown to bits already. On the positive side, we had made our mark on the Cretan landscape with a large and very expensive hole.

The next contractor would build a series of wooden-shuttering "moulds" up from the hole and pour all the cement necessary to give us solid foundations, a three-storey skeleton framework and all our flat roofs. This was vital work and a careful reading of Dimitris's plans and schedules for top-quality cement and metal reinforcing rods – intended to give the house the maximum protection against earthquakes – was a prime requirement. The first contractor we met, a self-important braggart, told us that he thought civil engineers were a waste of time and the second was a clod who obviously couldn't read the plans we set before him. We were in despair and then we met Antonis Vergerakis, from Kastelli, who we wished could have built the whole house for us. He did a magnificent job, going way beyond his contractual obligations and sorting out various problems for us. Buying materials was a major challenge. Back in England, I had once bought a small bag of cement from a DIY shop to bed-in a gatepost, but here we needed nearly 140 cubic metres of ready-mixed cement. Antonis cheerfully helped us deal with the purchase and 28 monster cement-mixer loads were brought to the site, together with a vast quantity of iron reinforcing rods. Dimitris visited the site to see that all was well and declared himself very happy with the work. This time we were also on schedule and within budget.

We couldn't spend all our time on the site: it was rather boring and builders' bottom is builders' bottom wherever you see it. We also had other things to do. For one thing, we had to show our faces in the *kafenea*... *Kafenea* play an important part in the social life of all Greek villages. They are the places to go for gossip, information – and to criticise the government. They also sell bottled beer, coffee, snacks and crisps, but – unlike English pubs – this is a matter of secondary importance. If you want to know something, ask at the *kafeneon*. Anyone looking for us had only to enquire at any of the *kafenea* in Afrata, upper or lower, and they would be told exactly where we were – and asked exactly what it was they wanted to see us about! It was in the Asteri that I fell into conversation with a foreigner from another village, a man who had been driving around in a car with German number plates for a lot longer than six months. "That's illegal," I said. "*Scheisse!*" he replied, as Germans frequently do, and then added, "You don't say?" I gave him the British Consulate's view of Greek car registration rules and he waved my commentary aside, "I know. I know. I don't give a damn for these stupid Greek car laws," he guffawed. I was heartened by his boldness and I felt defiance and hope surging in my 2CV-owner's breast. It was damped down as he went on to tell the whole story. He really didn't give a damn about Greek laws, but he covered himself, just in case. One trick was to buy the cheapest-possible ferry ticket every six months – but not to use it, unless you wanted to. Then, if you got stopped, you could produce the ticket and claim to have arrived in Crete on the day for which you had booked. "Clever, eh?" he said. "Yes..." I replied, uncertain of the economics underlying this manoeuvre but a rapid calculation showed me that in my case £3,500 would buy a lot of cheap ferry tickets. "If you get into really deep *scheisse*," he confided, "you can always get the number plates changed in Germany. These Greeks never notice." I mused on this and then asked him: "What are you doing here? You don't seem to have a very high opinion of Greeks." His answer was probably what many of his compatriots think. "Because Greece is the last free country in Europe. You can do what you like here," he said. "Can you get away with flouting rules in Germany?" I asked. "You must be kidding!" he snorted.

The electrician and the plumber had finished their preliminary work at the site just as the cement was about to be poured. The cement was now set – an event marked by an impromptu drinks party in the rough-and-ready basement – and we needed a bricklayer, a plasterer and a carpenter. Antonis had introduced his brother-in-law to us, yet another Antonis. We couldn't find any other bricklayers or plasterers to give us quotes and so the two jobs went to him by default. It was a happy accident. A trio of brickies-cum-plasterers turned up, led by Antonis. They were a jolly gang and they convinced us that it really didn't matter if some things weren't absolutely straight. Our carpenter and his mate were a more serious pair, though, apparently made so by the depressing quality of a lot of the timber they had to work with. Brickwork, plastering and woodwork went ahead while we took time off to look around for knobs and knockers and suchlike.

Kastelli was the sort of place that never had quite what you wanted – except for lunch. Everything was either too big or too small or it was available only in "avocado" or maroon-and-grey. If by some miracle, a shop had the right size and the right colour, it would invariably be chipped or cracked or missing some vital component. It was just like shopping in east Kent. Hania was the nearest place with decent shops, although by English standards most of them were on the small side. Despite this they kept extensive stocks, although where they kept them was always a bit of a mystery. But we weren't just shopping for the new house... We also visited the *laïki*, Hania's popular thrice-weekly street market, where the smell of fresh fruit and veg permeated the air around other stalls festooned with monumental brassieres for bargain-hunting matrons. The market sold jars of honey but, despite the piles of citrus fruit, no marmalade. I hadn't yet broken with my English habit of marmalade for breakfast and we were delighted to stumble upon a store near the market that sold jars of "Olde English". As I came out of the shop, an elderly lady poked me with her umbrella and asked me if I was an Albanian. I pointed to the marmalade and told her I was English. "Never mind," she said ambiguously and waddled off. "What was that all about?" I asked Susan. She just laughed and said that the old woman probably thought I was a likely looking lad to scrub out her cesspit in return for lunch and a few thousand drachmas. I decided it was more likely because, in the interests of economy, I'd let Susan cut my hair. The top of my head felt like moleskin after she'd finished with the clippers.

The lorry-boys had been around Afrata in our absence. At the Kali Kardia, one of the regulars was wearing a new lime-green sweatshirt with the words "TOTAL RELAXING OXFORD GEARS" pulsating across it in orange. I felt a migraine coming on as I stared at this meaningless slogan. Kostis had bought the absent Georgia a pair of shoes – in light brown plastic – but was now beginning to doubt that she'd like them, even if they fitted. She didn't. "Are you interested in buying some olives, Antoni?" asked Kostis. "Not if they came off the back of a lorry!" said Susan. "No, I mean some olive *trees*. I've got a friend who wants to sell his field," he explained. You can walk all around Afrata, which outside the village centre consists mainly of olive groves or rough pasture, the only obstacle being an occasional crude gate, usually made from an old iron bedstead in *arte povera* style. If you can get this open without injuring yourself, and refasten it, you can roam at will over private land, no one minds. We knew the grove that Kostis's friend wanted to sell; it had been neglected, apart from some fine old trees close to a track, and we often walked there with the pugs, who loved it. It was quiet, wild and overgrown and it had splendid views. Never mind the olives, we'd buy it to play in! Kostis arranged for us to meet his friend. The asking price was too high, but we all knew that. Our offer was too low, and we all knew that as well. So far, so good; everything was going as it should. There was even said to be a German hovering in the background who would, without a doubt, pay vastly more than the asking price... What made the land particularly interesting was that the owner claimed it was more than four *stremata* in size and this meant that one might be able to build on it – legally, that is. It was a beautiful site and this possibility would make it a good investment. We paid Dimitris to survey it; his report showed that it was less than four *stremata*. Before we could put this singular fact to the seller, he claimed that his German had come out of the woodwork and offered twice what we had proposed but that he would still sell it to us if we would improve our offer "a little". This bizarre demonstration of Cretan commercial illogicality left us unmoved. It had become an iron rule of ours never to believe in "Germans". When we showed the seller Dimitris's survey he was completely unmoved. "Ah, but size doesn't matter! When I said it was more than four *stremata* I didn't actually mean that it was more than four *stremata*," he explained. "That's alright," said Susan. "When we said we'd pay you two-and-a-half million drachmas, we didn't actually mean that we would actually pay you two-and-a-half million drachmas." And there the negotiations came to a halt. The German waiting in the wings didn't step forward either. The news that we were "looking for olives" went around Afrata and for weeks after villagers would sidle up to us and whisper "for sale" details in our ears. In the end we never did buy an olive grove of our own. We preferred to buy our olive oil directly from someone in the village; it was cheap enough and we by-passed the hassle of employing itinerant "Balkanian" labourers to help us with the hard and dirty work of harvesting our crop.

What had started off as a picturesque plot of land with an old stone-and-rubble shack now looked like a demolition site. Everything had a raw appearance and it wasn't clear whether a building was going up or coming down. What would eventually become a flourishing and colourful garden full of trees, flowers and vegetables was a muddy mess of rubble, broken palettes, beer bottles and cigarette packets. We only suffered one theft – someone came in the night and took 15 empty palettes that I had intended to chop up and use in the Norwegian wood-burning stove we had brought from England. On the other hand, the work was proceeding well, although the pace had slowed and our hopes of completing the job in "a few months" were not going to be fulfilled. We cast our minds forward to the matter of floors. Susan wanted *mosaico* – marble-chippings set within solid marble strips in a special cement and then ground down and polished. Once, this had been the most common – and practical – Greek flooring but then it went out of fashion, along with most of the craftsmen who knew how to do the job properly. The first flooring-contractor who came to see us was emphatic: *mosaico* couldn't be done because the materials were no longer available. He actually said: "You just can't get the chippings these days." According to him, we would have to have tiles, just like all his other customers. He was insistent, but we didn't believe him; we had seen *mosaico* being laid in Hania and we didn't want tiles, except in the bathrooms. In Crete, it pays to be persistent. We eventually found a craftsman who was reviving the vanishing art of *mosaico*. His workmanship impressed everyone. At first he had balked at the acute angles in the marble-strips of my floor-pattern but we persisted – as we knew we had to to get we wanted – and he succeeded, much to his own satisfaction and ours.

The flooring-contractor, like lots of people in the building trade, employed a foreign worker. His name was Spartakus and he had come to Greece from Georgia, in the Caucasus. Like most of the people we met from the former Soviet bloc, he mourned the passing of communism. "People here think that we had nothing," he told me. "The truth is that we had jobs and all the things that made life comfortable. Some Greeks I've met were astonished to learn that we even had fridges in our kitchens back home!" We also spoke to Romanians and Bulgarians who similarly felt that the communist collapse in their own countries had robbed them of the chance of a decent life. Their loss was usually described in practical rather than political terms. It seemed that, in the brave new world of the market economy, ushered in by *glasnost* and *perestroika*, the workers of the former eastern bloc had nothing to lose but their fridges – which, it seemed, they invariably did! History had apparently ensured that the Albanians always got the mucky end of the stick. They were poor wretches under communism, and they remained poor wretches in democratic Greece. They were even looked down upon by the other foreign workers in Crete. But the people looking for day-work at subsistence rates of pay didn't come only from eastern Europe. In Kastelli one day, we heard a man asking where he could find "the English field workers". Our ears pricked up. Was he talking about archaeology students on a dig? The question was quickly answered. Across the road a little group of grungy, indigent youths sat dejectedly near the unemployed "Balkanians". They were English and they too were jobless. They were looking for a field to work in; the man seeking them had several waiting. We watched as they enthusiastically clambered into the back of his farm truck to go and work for 8,000 drachmas a day. Was this what "mobility of labour" meant in the new Europe? And despite all the trumpeting about "harmonisation" of the rules to make job-hunting easier, we met a very put-out young Englishwoman in Hania who said she had just had to prove that she was free from venereal disease before she could get a permit to work in a private school. "I'm going to teach English grammar – not 69 positions from the *Kama Sutra!*" she declared.

CHAPTER SIXTEEN

It was the first day of the month and the customary good wishes for the weeks ahead – *"kalo mina"* – were on everybody's lips. It was also raining and very windy. Our builders didn't like working on our high and exposed site in such weather – which they hyperbolically described as "atrocious". I noticed that they kept a fortifying bottle of *tschikoudia* in their toolbag. They had colonised a piece of scrubby land in front of our plot and they daily parked their truck on it, alongside their cement mixer, piles of bricks, sand and gravel, tarpaulin-covered pyramids of cement – and a growing mound of rubbish. Along the side of our plot ran a narrow footpath, which led nowhere in particular – in fact it came to a dead end after a short distance. The owner of a small uncultivated field alongside this footpath had convinced himself that we were going to demolish the old dry-stone wall that marked our boundary and give over a strip of land so that a proper road could be built to replace the footpath. He might just as well have wished for a helicopter landing-pad because we had no intention of removing a very attractive old wall and surrendering land for such an unnecessary purpose. As it stood, he could drive to within about three yards of the boundary of his pocket-handkerchief of a field.

A second field-owner had also convinced himself that we would be demolishing our walls and handing over land to allow a road to be built. Perhaps they had persuaded each other that this would happen – although why they hadn't raised the subject when Kyriacos owned the land was a puzzle to us. When each of them realised that we weren't going to budge, they separately claimed ownership of the land that our builders were using at the front and threatened to stop them from doing so. The noise of the ensuing ding-dong echoing around the village brought more people to our site, each of them claiming something or the other and also threatening to make access to our house as difficult as possible. One even threatened to fence off the actual track that led up to our house while another accused us of kidnapping a tree! We turned to

Kyriacos and to Manolis Kekakis, the village president, our "mayor", for help. Kyriacos pointed out that the tree in question had belonged to his mother – which made it very old because he was 74! – and anyway it was clearly on our property, while Manolis, who was regularly called upon to be the village peacemaker, pointed out that the agricultural track was a public road. The troublemakers retreated. Nevertheless, it hadn't been a good start to a new month.

Within the course of the month, we came face-to-face with each of the people we had argued with. They all acknowledged us either with a curt nod or a formally polite greeting. This didn't mean that we were all friends. In fact we were far from well-disposed towards them; they had gratuitously caused a lot of distress and I referred to them accordingly – forever after they were known to me as "The *Malákia*", which I later discovered meant "molluscs". This wasn't the word I had wanted! Nevertheless, life in the village had to go on. In Crete, even after a blazing row, most people – other than northern European incomers who can't change the habits of a lifetime – will still acknowledge each other when they meet in public. And that's how it was with us. It was infinitely better than the English way of stony silence, carefully plotted point-scoring and festering resentment. I remembered an experience I'd had when I lived in Broadstairs. Someone had posted an anonymous note, written in green ballpoint ink, through my front door: "This was a nice place until you came. Go back where you came from and take your gas van with you." I had had a house in the town for 18 years – and the reference to my "gas van" baffles me still.

Predictably, news of our little local difficulty had percolated through to the *kafeneon*, where it had obviously been discussed in detail by the regulars. Several old codgers, all obviously from an "anti-mollusc" faction, took me to one side to tell me that over the years they had heard so many people claim different things about the scrap of land in front of us that they didn't believe it was worth worrying about. Nothing would ever happen there – except occasional rows. The truth was out there somewhere, but we couldn't find it. What amazed us was that when the telephone and electricity cables were brought to the house, huge timber poles were plonked right in the middle of the argued-over land, blighting it for all time. Nobody had given permission for this to happen – and no one appeared even to notice the arrival of the monstrous poles!

There was a postscript to this story – a predictable one. Shortly after the initial confrontation we were offered one of the fields close to our house. The asking price was six million drachmas and it was said to be more than four *stremata* in size, which it patently wasn't. We said we'd pay one million drachmas for it. Hermann-the-mythical-German was still on cue, hovering in the wings. He was said to be prepared to pay nine million drachmas but – and we knew what was coming – we could have it if we agreed to pay the six... We didn't buy the field, but then neither did Hermann.

Electricity had arrived in Afrata in 1967, by overhead line, but it had been an irregular visitor ever since and this wet and windy month was particularly bad. Power cuts were frequent and sometimes lengthy, and just like train cancellations and slow-running on Britain's railways a variety of excuses were trotted out to explain the appalling service. "Sparrow droppings" was the best one we ever heard. Back in the summer, not long after we had arrived in the village, there was a power cut lasting more than 30 hours, but that was unusual – most lasted only for an hour or two. That day-and-a-half's loss of electricity was a dreadful event for the village's two competing *kafenea* – the Kali Kardia and the Asteri. They lost their stocks of ice cream and thus the main weapons in their armouries for enticing passers-by on to their respective terraces. It was Dick Stringer, the Englishman who maintained a holiday-home in upper Afrata, who had observed that the village saw only two types of tourist: "There are those who drive up the mountain, stop for an ice-cream, turn around and drive down again – and those who drive up, turn around and drive down again." Afrata would have been a darker place without Dick, a retired army officer, who administered one of the City of London's ancient guilds. After every banquet organised by the guild there was always a box of half-burnt candles that were useless for the next feast and that a less-thrifty person would have allowed to be thrown away. Many's the time we've sat power-less in a blacked-out Afrata and drunk a glass of wine by the light of one of Colonel Dick's salvaged second-hand candles!

An unexpected telephone call brought Melkhizedek back to mind. The call was from Hamburg, from Gertie, the German artist who was so inspired by the atmosphere at the Rotonda, Melkhizedek's church. "I have been telephoning Melkhizedek, and I can get no answer. I don't understand why he is not there. Will you please go to the Rotonda and see what has happened," she pleaded. I didn't know that monks had telephones; I wondered if it was a mobile. Gertie sounded so concerned that I didn't have the heart to refuse her. I promised to go the next day... As I parked the car by the church I noticed a pair of underpants swinging on a washing line behind the church. I thought that if they were Melkhizedek's it was a good sign. After a monkish vow of poverty, he was unlikely to have more than two or three pairs – not enough to be able to afford to abandon one of them. Unfortunately, the church door was locked. All was very quiet. I would have little to report to Gertie that evening.

Gertie rang on the dot of seven, as she said she would. "Well, all I saw was a pair of...er...washing on the line. The church was locked up," I told her. "Oh dear!" she said. "You know I telephoned a friend of mine in Germany. He is a retired optician. I asked him if he thought Melkhizedek had left. He said that as far as he could see, no he hadn't. What do you think, Tony?" she asked. Well, Afrata was much nearer to the Rotonda than Germany was, but I couldn't see the situation any more clearly than the retired optician. Melkhizedek had hinted that he thought his superiors might have other plans for him but that his first love was St Michael and the Rotonda, where he wanted to stay. Susan and I went to the Rotonda three or four times in as many weeks; it remained locked and the underpants, by now thoroughly rinsed by the persistent rain, still swung on the line. Those pants were the last – and rather ironic – reminder of Melkhizedek. I, for one, missed his cheerful countenance at the gloomy old church.

It seemed that every day we had to buy something or other for the house. We always dreaded returning to Afrata with any purchases because it didn't matter what we'd bought, whoever was looking at it always knew someone who'd have let us have it for less. This didn't seem to apply to bricks and such-like, though. Fortunately for us, there was a builder's merchant in Kolymbari, who could supply – and deliver – most of what we needed. The 2CV was a sterling little workhorse, but there was a limit to the number of sacks of cement its 602cc engine could pull up the mountain road to Afrata. Customers calling into the office at the Diakoulakis yard were greeted by a sign advising that the firm did not give credit and that all building materials had to be paid for on the spot. We were complete strangers when we walked in there with a shopping list prepared by Antonis the bricklayer. "Do you want to pay now – or shall I put it on your account?" asked the friendly clerk. Our account? "On the account, please," I said, fully expecting him to tap the keyboard of his computer and then say, "Oh! I thought you were someone else..." But he didn't. Two words – "Cox" and "Afrata" – were all that he needed to know. In fact, that's all anyone needs to know to be able find us!

Everywhere we went we found our bills rounded down or unexpected discounts given. We were seldom charged for small single items, such as a chrome shower-curtain hook, in shops where we were known and sometimes we were given even more: the electrical shop we used in Hania let us have three plugs free-of-charge. This seemed quite common behaviour. We had been in the Tzitzikas taverna one lunchtime the previous summer when an English couple wandered in. "Do you take Eurocheques?" Katina's son Elias was asked. "No. Only cash," he answered. The two hungry faces fell; they didn't have any and the nearest bank was a 20-minute drive away. "Are you staying around here?" asked Elias. They were. "Then please have what you want and come and pay us tomorrow," offered the friendly young Elias. This was too much for the English pair, who frantically searched their minds for the catch. They obviously couldn't find one and so they sat down and ate. A few weeks later, we asked Elias what happened. "Oh, yes," he recalled. "Nice couple – they had dinner here for ten nights in a row!" Elias knew his business.

Walking through Hania one day I saw an advertisement stapled to a telegraph pole. Cretans regularly use telegraph poles in this way. The one in the centre of Afrata always has details of funerals or memorial services nailed to it. The advertisement offered Greek language classes – something I desperately needed.

The first lesson was memorable. Angela, the teacher, greeted the assembled class. It sounded like the start of a joke: there was an Irishwoman, a Dutchman, two Englishmen and a Chinese... We started off by introducing ourselves and saying where we came from. The Chinese didn't seem to speak English – as the rest of us did – and Angela was thin on Mandarin. After half-an-hour of us all expectantly willing him to articulate something we could understand, the Chinese stood up, bowed and said, "Souda." At least that's what the others claimed he said. I thought it might have been a strangulated attempt at, "Sod it!" Anyway, we never saw him again. Maybe he took a slow boat back home – the ferries sailed from Souda! The classes proceeded and I became friends with Tara, Gert-Jahn and Ian, my compatriot. Later we were joined by Barbara, a German who could obviously already speak a lot of Greek. I asked her why she was attending the classes. "I have big holes," she said. I shouldn't have laughed; I had my own difficulties. Greek's an easy language to make mistakes in and I was in the class because instead of telling a petrol attendant to "fill her up" I had come very close to using the Greek "f" word! Step by slow step, Angela coaxed us through to the end of book one of the course but, although she did her best, I never felt really confident when buying petrol.

It seemed to be a month for burials. Afrata's telegraph pole was displaying three funeral notices. One of them was for an old man we had spoken to often enough to think that we should join the mourners. Nick telephoned to say that he was going to take two of his American students to the same funeral. I knew that he liked to be able to offer them real-life, hands-on experiences whenever possible and a convenient funeral was just the ticket for their "anthropology" course. It was a big funeral and the churchyard was packed with mourners. As was usual, most of the women went inside the church, while most of the men sat around outside chatting, smoking and playing with their worry-beads. We were sitting on the churchyard wall next to two aged villagers, while Nick, his wife and the two students stood just in front of us. The old man sitting next to me turned to his friend, gestured at the foursome standing alone and asked: "Who are these people?" His friend adjusted his glasses and peered at them. "Tourists," he said dismissively. Funerals, baptisms, weddings and memorial services are frequent events in the local churches, but for an unredeemed bellower of *Hymns Ancient & Modern*, like myself, there's not much to do in a Greek Orthodox religious service, where the congregation mostly just spectates, and I no longer put in an appearance unless I have to. I usually attend on the third day of November though because I have a vested interest in the outcome. That's when the villagers take a sample of their new wine to the church and ask St George for his blessing on it. They also get an off-the-vestment crit from the priest, who samples every supplicant's offering!

The structure of our new house was now evident. It rose from the hole in the ground as an unsightly block of cement, raw bricks and iron rods, looking more like a second world war gun emplacement than the white island-style house we had planned. I had salvaged the traditional dressed stones from Turnip's demolished stable and now I planned to use them to construct some external walling. Unfortunately, I didn't have enough. Antonis the bricklayer knew someone with a pile of them, and he said he would ask if I could have a few. I could – but at 3,000 drachmas each. Antonis pooh-poohed this price with such vigour that I really didn't think I could say, "Could you get me half-a-dozen?" Instead, I went looking for them in the various rubbish dumps that dotted the area. I found 60,000 drachmas' worth. It had been worth the trouble. Alongside a dead sheep, two ruptured mattresses and half-a-dozen three-legged plastic garden chairs, I rediscovered the gates and the garden seat that I had turned up all those months ago. I arranged for Aristides to collect and repair them and bring them to the house site. Obviously, there was a slow turnover of local rubbish! These tips became important to me because there was nowhere in Hania which equalled a traditional English junk shop. In fact, those old junk shops were my favourite stamping ground and they remain the one thing that I feel deeply nostalgic about. Hania had places selling "antiques" but, with my budget, they were of little use to me. I found many interesting old things in the rubbish – bits of a pistol, bottles, door locks, a washboard, wooden boxes, letters... It was like the old-style *News of the World* slogan: "All human life is here." I had a list of wants, at the top of which was a traditional Cretan brass doorknocker: a little hand grasping a ball. I felt sure that sooner or later someone would throw out an old door with the "furniture" on it. I'm still looking! My best find was two robust old *kafeneon* chairs, in good condition except that their rush-bottoms had long since dropped out. I cleaned them up and got the local chair repairer to re-seat them both for 6,000 drachmas. This kind of bargain hunting had become my hobby. Only once did I ever meet anyone else rummaging around a rubbish tip; he was looking for some lengths of plastic drainpipe. The Cretans who saw me obviously thought I was like one of those poor demented souls who wander around, wild-eyed and muttering, wearing too-short trousers and carrying bulging plastic carrier bags full of dirty old newspapers.

Kostis made an exciting find towards the end of the month – but not on a rubbish tip. Summertime visitors would never believe the storms that we get in the winter months. The sea can become so wild that ships are forced to anchor close in to Kolymbari to ride out the dreadful weather. After one such storm, there appeared to be snow on the rocks along the edge of the sea, midway between Afrata and Kolymbari. It was Kostis, driving past in his truck on one of his regular journeys between the two villages, who noticed it and clambered down to investigate. It was desiccated coconut, unfortunately by now a little salty. However, further searching revealed undamaged sacks of the stuff littering the rocks. Kostis salvaged what he could and took it back up to Afrata, where he set himself up as a one-man relief agency doling out desiccated coconut to all who needed it. There was so much coconut in Afrata that people started to feed it to their animals. For weeks, an Afratan roast chicken would have a distinctly tropical flavour and people were forever looking for new ways to use up this unexpected bounty. Susan suggested that there were plenty of

Indian dishes that would take a sprinkle of coconut but Cretans are unadventurous eaters and boiled mutton was hot enough for them without turning it into a vindaloo. The coconut had come from a container ship that had been hit by the stormy weather. Afterwards, everyone kept an eye on those rocks, just in case.

The postman, Nikos, delivers mail to houses in the centre of Afrata but out-of-the-village houses either have to collect letters from one of the *kafenea* or from the post office in Kolymbari, where they're put in a grubby old cardboard box officially labelled *"Poste Restante"* and kept on a shelf by the postmaster's desk. I did not believe people's warnings that once in Crete we would be plagued with letters from people wanting to come and stay – and certainly not before we had a house of our own with a guest room. The first threatening letter we had was from someone I hadn't seen for five years, although we always exchanged Christmas cards. His letter came in response to the change-of-address note I had written in the Christmas card. Probably spurred on by the approach of Easter, his letter started with, "We love Crete and we'd like to come and see you…" and then quite boldly moved on to, "How would you be placed for putting up the two of us and Imogen, who's now a truculent toddler (!)? We'd stay for two weeks…" I didn't reply, although I left his name on the Christmas card list. A few more letters like that made me realise just how crass some people can be. It's amazing how "friends" who couldn't drive for 30 minutes to see you in England will happily endure an interminable and sweaty night-time charter flight to spend two weeks in and out of your fridge once it's been plugged in next to the Mediterranean! I blew a gasket when a notorious sponging freeloader of my acquaintance announced that he liked to make his summer holiday arrangements well in advance. He wanted to know when our new house would be ready. I sent him a postcard recommending that he stripped down to his poser's pouch, smeared himself with honey and stretched out on Clapham Common, where someone – and in all probability someone who'd been on a sunny beach the week before – would be bound to stick to him. That way he'd save himself the expensive high-season airfare and end up with the same likely result. He replied with a three-page letter cataloguing his multiple acts of generosity to a string of impoverished young actresses.

We weren't without visitors, though. As the weeks rolled by we met various people, either by chance or introduction. The villagers were always curious about the people who came to see us in our flat on the *plateia*, particularly if they were blonde – and female. Emmeline had come from King's College, London, to study for a year in Rethimnon, and she was weary of the noisy attention her long blonde hair frequently attracted from swarthy Cretan "harpoonists" constantly on the lookout for foreign women seeking holiday romance. Her arrival at our front door was rapidly followed by a visit from one of Afrata's moustache-stroking Lotharios. "Antoni!" he exclaimed. "Yes?" I asked. He ran his eye over our visitor, smiled and said, "Er...there's a man here selling chestnuts." Jo, an English teacher in Kastelli, also became a regular visitor. She was blonde *and* tall – an irresistible combination for Crete's shortish-darkish males – and her first visit attracted two village moustache-strokers who didn't let any nonsense about chestnuts distract them.

I went up to our house site just as the lads were starting their *tschikoudia* break. They invited me to join them and although no one read out aloud from a rolled-up copy of *The Sun* I suspect that building workers in England enjoy much the same sort of conversation during their tea breaks. One of them was telling a story about a cunning German who was getting dole money sent from home but also took in washing to make some extra cash. When asked what kind of washing machine he had, the German had said, "A fat Bulgarian." The German was taking in the dirty laundry from some tavernas and then sub-contracting it to the Bulgarian. That way he got the money without doing the work. The Bulgarian, however, was equally cunning and just as lazy. One day the laundry wasn't ready and the German discovered that the Bulgarian had sub-sub-contracted it to an Albanian! It's hard to say who would be at the end of the line in this little parable of exploitation because queuing is virtually unheard of in Crete!

The month ended in sunshine but All Fools' Day was cloudy and saw the return of one of the troublemakers. "What is it now?" I barked; it was an English response, not a Greek one. "Do you want to buy any charcoal?" he asked. Easter was coming and every household would be needing charcoal to spit-roast the traditional lamb. I took his offer as a gesture that showed he saw us as villagers. I bought a sack-full, which he weighed in a rough-and-ready way. The weight was approximate – but then so was the handful of small notes and coins that I gave him. The charcoal's arrival was timely. Susan had remembered reading a story in which a farty hound was successfully treated with charcoal. Our dogs' flatulence had become embarrassing with the increasing number of visitors to our small flat. Not that we always pointed the finger at Pug and Mavros; for all we knew the guilty party might have been one of the visitors... I had kept an old dog-care book that recommended that flatulent dogs be given "brandy in a little water". We gave ours *tschikoudia* and they lapped it up, but the farting continued. We stopped the treatment when we realised we were at risk of having dogs who were both stinking *and* stinko. Susan fed them bits of charcoal, which blackened their crooked little teeth but never got to the bottom of their problem.

CHAPTER SEVENTEEN

We missed our first Greek Easter as resident Afratans. Susan had plugged us into the Internet and the service provider had put her name into a prize draw for new subscribers. For the first time in her life, her name came out of the hat. "We've won a long-weekend trip – to Paris!" she reported after a congratulatory 'phone call from the competition organiser. We went, leaving the pugs to chew their way through left-over lamb served up by Dimitra. Of course, we enjoyed the trip – we hadn't yet become complete peasants – but we were glad to get back to where we now felt that we belonged, Afrata. In Paris, we had particularly enjoyed the now-unusual experience of dining in smart restaurants – and being on the receiving end of the finesse of professional waiters – but we were both agreed that the tasty-enough *ragoût de porc aux poireaux* didn't match the robust flavour of the pork *stifado* casually delivered to the table at The Stork, in Kastelli, while a bottle of vintage Afratan *Château Platsaki* could easily hold its own against many pricey French labels.

One thing that didn't belong in Crete any longer was the 2CV, now sadly out of its "honeymoon" period. It had to go, not least because one of our new resident expat friends had painfully discovered that only *bona fide* tourists were now allowed to drive around Greece in cars sporting foreign registration plates. The concession allowing six months of "free circulation" had gone. In Greece, official goal posts move frequently; rules and regulations change with the seasons and one can never be certain that what was acceptable last week will still hold true next week. Our friend's parked car had been spotted by a roving patrol of customs officers – allegedly an elite hit squad collectively known as "Rambo" – and impounded after he failed to produce a bucket-and-spade and a deckchair. He was warned that he faced a huge fine for his disregard of a new bureaucratic law that few if any of the people it affected knew anything about – until it was too late. When he went to sort matters out, he was first given a slice of chocolate cake – because an official in the office was celebrating her name day – and then politely asked to take his car out of Greece within a week. The threatened fine somehow got overlooked. I told this story to the German who bought the ferry tickets to cover himself if his long-stay German-plated car ever came under scrutiny. "So what? I'm not worried," he said. "I always park right outside the customs office – they never notice anything stuck right under their nose!" We weren't prepared to take the risk and so our 2CV was sent away. The last I heard, it was still chugging away; around Slough, I believe. The car had served us so well that we bought another. It was a two-tone orange-and-rust Greek model to which even a crooked English back-street garage would never have given a dodgy MoT. It wasn't half the car we'd left England in, but it cost us nearly four times as much – which explains why foreigners like to keep their imported cars running for as long as possible. We bought it because mechanical and bodywork repairs are cheap in Crete. Our friendly Citroën mechanic in Hania, Yiannis Yereoudakis, made it roadworthy and we set off to take it – fingers crossed! – around the clock one more time.

The house was progressing, slowly. The sun shone every day and as the temperature rose so the progress appeared to slow. Rain or shine, the builders complained about the weather. They were good workers but they didn't seem to be setting any speed records. Apart from our first contractor, the JCB man, no one was paid by the hour so the job should have been proceeding at a rate of knots. It didn't often look like that! Sometimes, visiting the building site was like walking on to the set of a deep, brooding, existentialist French film. There was a heavy silence in which everything seemed to proceed in slow motion. When the weather was just right for them, the energised builders would sing Cretan songs together, sometimes jolly, sometimes melancholy. The truth was that they were actually working rather well, but there was so much work for them to do – a lot of it very fiddly – that progress was often difficult to judge. The most depressing part of the house-building process was the regular monthly visit to the IKA office to join the unruly and disorganised scrum of people wasting half-a-day trying to pay-in social security contributions on behalf of their workers. Well-dressed middle-class folk – all employed or in business – were reduced to pushing, shoving and shouting to try and get the clerks to approve their calculations. It was bizarre. Nothing could be done by post; everything had to be done in person. If it was like this for people trying to pay money *into* the system, I wondered what it was like for claimants, the poor sods trying to get some money *out* of the system. When we made our last payment, we had fresh swordfish steaks to celebrate!

In Hania one day we took a broken wristwatch to the mender. We followed an elderly peasant-farmer into the shop and watched him haul a large and ancient pocket watch from his jacket and hand it over. "It doesn't work," he said dolefully. The watch-mender opened the back and tapped the watch gently on his workbench. A little pile of earth fell out. "Have you been growing potatoes in here? When did it stop working?" he asked. The old man scratched his head: "About 10 years ago. I think..." The watchmender scratched his head. "So why bring it to me now?" he asked. "I thought it was about time," answered the old man. The watchmender shrugged. "Well, I can't repair it," he said. The old man also shrugged: "It doesn't matter." We were beginning to feel exactly the same. Time no longer mattered that much. If you were visiting someone and you made to leave, they'd invariably say, "Why are you going? Do you have an appointment?" A watch was useful for timing an egg or taking a pulse but was unnecessary most of the time. The pattern of life in Afrata really required a broader canvas than the face of a 12-hour clock. There was Christmas and the New Year and then Easter. In the autumn there was the grape-harvest and wine-treading and in the winter, olive-picking. Sheep and goats were there all year round. There were special church celebrations and national holidays, the best-known being *Oxi* – No! – Day, in October, which commemorated Greece's spirited defiance of the Italian fascist leader, Mussolini, at the start of the war. In the main, it was enough to follow the sun through its daily course and respond to the changes of the seasons.

Susan carved out a vegetable garden from land that the builders hadn't dumped anything on and studied to become a professionally-qualified Greek-into-English translator. She passed her exams and advertised her services. The first customer was a man who wanted to write to the Secretary of State for Health for the address of a reputable sex-change clinic in the UK. The next was a Greek student at a British breeze-block university. He wanted Susan to translate his dissertation into English – from English! His written English had proved impenetrable, even to tutors whose professional practice seldom required the use of the word "unacceptable". I wrote, did some drawing, studied Greek and repaired the broken things that I salvaged from the rubbish tip. We both spent a lot of time up at the house and we continued to enjoy our encounters with people.

I drew a charcoal portrait of Kyriacos. When Kostis saw it, he said, "Which one is he? The good, the bad or the ugly?" Later, he asked me to make him a new sign for the Kali Kardia. He wanted something with a large plate of egg and chips painted on it. I felt obliged to insist upon my artistic integrity. I offered to make him a sign, but to my own design. Competition for the slender tourist trade was hotting up between the two *kafenea* on the *plateia* and Kostis was looking for something to give him the edge over the Asteri. I suggested writing "tourist information" – in English – on the sign. "Good idea," he said, although I knew he couldn't speak a word of English. "What about, 'We speak German'?" I asked. He said I could put it on if I wanted to! I invented an angular Greek script and made him a huge sign. The first line read, "DRINKS MEALS SNACKS". Unfortunately, I hadn't experimented enough with the letter forms and the first day the sign was up I overheard two tourists read aloud, "Drinks, meals...and snakes?" Nevertheless, it did the trick for a while – that is, until the Asteri restored the balance by getting a new sign.

We hadn't been to the Tzitzikas for many weeks and we decided to have lunch there before the taverna became busy serving tourists. Elias greeted us warmly and said that only yesterday he'd said to his mother, Katina, that we hadn't been in for a long time. "She thought perhaps you'd gone abroad," said Elias. We enjoyed this unexpected compliment. It would, after all, have been quite different had he said, "She thought perhaps you'd gone home." There weren't many tourists in the taverna, but the *kafenea* in Afrata would have been glad to see half their number arrive in the village. We were always ready to speak to tourists in Afrata, unlike many expat residents who seemed to live in fear of encouraging them. Crete was an enviable place to be – particularly to people on a two-week break from suburbia – but it sometimes seemed that incomers wanted to pull up the drawbridge to stop anyone else coming in. They also looked down on tourists as somehow second-class – an opinion which explained those assertive "I'm not a tourist! I live here!" T-shirts. On the other hand, in unenviable places there was probably a living to be made selling T-shirts saying, "I don't *live* here! I'm only a tourist!"

Most tourists said they envied us our escape from England, but not all. When visitors discovered that we lived in the village all year round, the comment would either be a variant of, "You lucky bastards!" or it would be, "What on earth do you do with yourselves all day long?" There were more of the former than the latter, but the latter was closer to the mark. We had plenty to do – from writing letters about sex-change operations to making confusing signboards! – and plenty of time for ourselves, but I could see that for a great many people a new life on the Rodopou peninsula would be like exile to a gulag of lonely desolation. Included among such unhappy folk would be some of the people who sincerely said that they envied us. They weren't focused on the reality of life here; they were getting a distorted view through their Cretan rosé-tinted wine glasses! No one should come here on a whim. Doctors use the Survey of Recent Experiences to assess a patient's risk of developing a major illness. The survey lists 43 "life changes" which can add up to disaster for some people. The list includes retirement – the tenth most serious item – and changes in income, living conditions, personal habits, residence, recreational and social activities and eating habits. That brief catalogue would be the absolute minimum number of life changes for most people retiring to Crete.

Our eating habits were definitely undergoing a sea change – we were eating far more fresh fish! In England we hadn't eaten fish more than once a month; now it was a twice-weekly dish. It was the meat, however, that continued to present the biggest challenge. Walking past Themis's house one day I saw him plunging his hands in and out of what looked like a bucket of green pea soup. He was washing out a sheep's intestines. "Are you going to put them back when they're clean?" I asked. "What?" he replied. He was making *kokoretsi* – lambs innards sausages. I moved on before he could invite me to join him for lunch. Back at the flat I told Susan what I had seen. "Yummy!" she said. "I love *kokoretsi.* I've got a recipe here somewhere..." She rummaged among her cookery books and read out: "First, carefully trim off and discard all the fat, membranes, sinews and valves from the offal..." I saw another Greek delicacy loom before me. "I can't wait," I lied.

The summer months were very hot but we invariably enjoyed a breeze at this height above sea level. Nevertheless, it was uncomfortable for some elderly villagers, including Antonia, who had developed a heart problem. We asked her how old she was, but she would say only that she was younger than Yiannis, her next-door neighbour. One evening, when it was intolerably hot in the cramped flat, we went for a walk along the mountain road where we had first met Yiannis. He was there now, throwing stones in the direction of his sheep and swearing vigorously at them. "They're being naughty girls!" he explained. He sat down on his favourite rock – from where he had once watched screaming dive-bombers attack the allied defenders of the Maleme airfield down below – and asked us if we knew much about hedgehogs. "Not much. Why?" I asked. "I've just found a dead one in my pear tree," said a genuinely puzzled Yiannis. Susan asked him if he knew how old Antonia was. "It's one of Afrata's mysteries," he said, "but I know she's older than I am because when I was just a little boy she already had big breasts!"

It got hotter and we were plagued with flies. We vigorously whacked our way through a couple of plastic fly-swats every week for a month. In the oppressive heat of Hania, freshly-squeezed orange juice was selling for 600 or more drachmas a glass in the tourist cafés. Nevertheless, growers like Georgis Dagounakis, Yiannis's son, were finding it difficult to sell their crop. Georgis owned a large orange grove not far from Kolymbari. "Pick as many as you want – as often as you want," he told us. We took him at his word and gathered bags of juicy oranges whenever we needed them. The orange glut got so bad that lorry-loads of unsaleable oranges were dumped on the mountainsides for the goats to nibble at. Antonia was having a similar problem with the many lemon trees in her garden. "Help yourselves to lemons," she said when we called in to see if we could do anything for her. She went on to ask us to collect some medicine for her from the chemist's shop in Kolymbari. To do this we had to have her prescription book, on the cover of which were her personal details. The mystery was solved. She was 92.

There were a lot of dogs in Afrata – and a goodly number of cats – but just one donkey, which belonged to the aged Stratis. In the past donkeys had been common; they were the only means of transport up and down the mountain track. Petrula remembered the birth of her son Georgis. It had been a difficult labour and after three days of suffering, she relented and agreed to have the doctor up from Kolymbari. The doctor's plodding little donkey had just reached the Platsakis's house as Petrula's baby arrived safely under its own steam. "So you didn't need the doctor?" Susan said. "No! But he charged us nonetheless," said Petrula, with whom the bill still obviously rankled.

The weeks rolled on, the house progressed. The summer began to fade, ever so slightly, and we harvested and trod grapes with our village friends. Yiannis bought a piglet to fatten up for Christmas. He named it "Mitsotakis", after a right-wing Greek politician. In December, said Yiannis, the unfortunate porker would be promoted to "The Prime Minister"! In November we went to church to add our prayers for more good wine. Christmas came and we enjoyed a slice of Mitsotakis with our friends. Another New Year was greeted by pistol shots and fireworks. Olive trees were thwacked and the crop carted off for pressing. Wet weather delayed our building work.

The house was completed exactly one year after we had started the demolition of Turnip's old stable. And we had thought it would take a few months! It had also cost much more than we had anticipated and it would now be a waste of time for villagers to try and sell us olive groves. We had nothing left – except for a very fine house, which could be seen from miles around – and from which we could see that we had done the right thing.

We were probably the only people in western Crete sitting outside with a glass of wine on that last day of February. It wasn't cold enough to deny us the pleasure of sitting on our terrace in the knowledge that it was now ours, and ours alone. The builders had gone. We sat together – with Pug and Mavros – on the old garden seat that I had salvaged from the rubbish tip. From the terrace we marvelled at the snow-capped peaks of the majestic White Mountains range and enjoyed the melodious tinkling sound of distant goat-bells travelling sharp and clear through the limpid air...

Our enjoyment was short-lived. "Antoni! Susannah!" It was Andreas, a short, squat shepherd with a foghorn voice, who could be hired as a sort of village crier to wander around shouting out invitations. He didn't need a bell. He stood at our front gates and bellowed that we were invited to a wedding. "Thank you, Andrea," I shouted back to him, "but we don't know the couple getting married." He waved, yelled, "Never mind! That doesn't matter!" – and took himself off to shout at someone else.

The stillness returned to our terrace and the goat-bells could be heard again. In the distance two huge helicopters silently hovered over the sea, just off Maleme. We watched as parachutists tumbled out and floated down. We would have seen much the same thing had we been sitting here in 1941. Then the doorbell rang. Whoever it was, it definitely wasn't a Cretan. Susan looked over the terrace wall. Down below was a German woman who often stayed at a house in the village. We knew who she was but the only time our paths ever crossed was when her car passed ours on the Kolymbari road. "Hello there," said Susan. "Hello," said the German woman. "I bring you bread and salt. It is a German tradition when people move into a new house." I joined Susan at the wall and we invited our unexpected visitor to join us, but she wouldn't. "Never mind," I said. We returned to our seat, tuned in once again to the sound of the goat-bells, and waited...

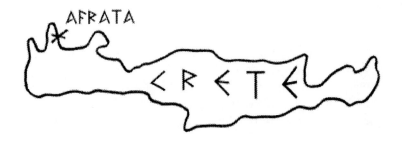

P.S.

I finished my manuscript and blithely thought, "Well, that's the end of that." My prescience was remarkable! The optimism with which I packaged up my completed manuscript and launched it on the first of its 19 journeys into the literary world was soon blunted. They were all to be return journeys! My opus was invariably the largest item awaiting collection from Kolymbari post office's battered *poste restante* box and the clerk's bantering remarks suggested that he knew a rejected manuscript when he saw one. When I gave an interim lack-of-progress report to a friend who had long since recycled the manuscript of his first – and last – novel, he exclaimed, "Only 18? You've got a long way to go!" His manuscript had acquired more than 30 rejections and he was bizarrely proud of them all. When Literary Agent No.19 bluntly informed me that "nobody is interested in Crete and nobody knows you – so nobody will buy your book", I was ready to agree with him. I decided that my Cretan tale had reached its end. *Still Life in Crete* would not be getting a twentieth trip anywhere!

Then I happened upon a magazine article about downloadable e-books, the "latest thing" in publishing (even work by Stephen King and Frederick Forsyth has appeared in electronic format) and I realised that with Susan's help I could, at no great expense, become an international publisher on the World Wide Web. Together we created *inkmonitor.com* (all the better domain names having long since gone). I would have nothing on paper, of course

190

– unlike my e-peers, Messrs King and Forsyth – but at least my words would forever be just a mouse-click away from anyone who *might* want to read them. It was a better prospect than allowing them to moulder at the back of my government-surplus filing cabinet. While I was surfing the net for more information about e-books I discovered, by chance, the publishing world's next "latest thing", print-on-demand (POD) technology – which makes it possible to publish a book without printing a single copy until somebody wants one! Each copy is truly "hot off the press" because it is printed *on demand*. If no one wants to read your book, then no copies will be printed. If 98,462 people want it, then 98,462 copies will be printed. No POD book will ever go out of print, or be remaindered, because the stock is created day-by-day, year after year, to meet actual demand. Freed from the burden of printing and storing books in advance of sales, "new technology" firms can take on titles – and unknown authors – that conventional publishers would reject out of hand.

Without Susan's help my book would never have made it on to any screen other than my own; without Universal, my POD-publishing house, *Still Life in Crete* would never have appeared as a paperback. I thank them both. These expressions of gratitude would be incomplete without a mention of Geoff Cox, my bibliophilic son, who directed me on to the straight and narrow of authorship by successfully dissuading me from pursuing *some* of my foolish ways. If I have strayed too far, it is my own fault.

I am still Literary Agent No.19's "nobody", of course, but if you've got this far you've proved him wrong in two respects: you were interested *and* you did buy the book. I hope I'm right on both counts! Of course, I didn't send my manuscript to every agent in London, but would the response have been any different if I'd sent it to 90 rather than 19? I doubt it. Not one of the 19 had said my manuscript was badly written...

Now, back to Afrata, where many things have happened since that blithe typing of "The End" on the last page of my manuscript. There couldn't be a grand final full stop to any account of life in a Cretan village – at least, not until the last trump! Antonia

Kalitsaki died. Everyone had expected her to make 100, but her heart let her down. A niece came from Athens and moved into the old lady's house – together with four dogs and a parrot. The quiet footpath became a cacophonous gauntlet to be run. Dieter, the German from Israel, finished his conversion of the olive mill, which he moved into with his teenage daughter. The building received mixed reviews from Afrata's resident architectural critics. Its mock crazy-paving and "pebbledashed" walls reminded me of an English suburban semi in "South London Tyrolean" style; on the other hand, most villagers claimed it was "very nice". Beauty, of course, is in the eye of the beholder! While the old olive mill may now look, to me at least, like a fat tea-stained finger, it definitely doesn't beckon passers-by with quite the same visual force as Nick's house, which is the first building you'll see as you drive round the bend into "Outer Afrata". One day the house was painted a subdued creamy colour, the next it looked like a vividly embarrassed pumpkin. Maybe it'll have changed again before you visit... Greek local government was reformed and Afrata lost its status as a semi-autonomous parish. More importantly, it seemed to lose whatever clout it had once had in the upper reaches of the lower-levels of public administration. The villagers moaned that never again would anything be done for Afrata. We hope they're wrong. The public road to our house is deteriorating so rapidly that soon it will be impassable without the aid of ropes and crampons. Despite repeated visits to the new district council offices in Kolymbari, where such things are supposedly now dealt with, the only answer we can get is the usual Greek one, which is, more-or-less, "Tomorrow – or maybe the day after..." Nick's teenage son left the village for boarding school in America... Robin and Pat arrived totally unexpectedly from Harwich, in Essex, and, without a word of Greek between them, bought a small olive grove midway between Upper and Lower Afrata. Their plan was to build a bungalow, with an underground garage for their vintage Rolls-Royce, and open a small restaurant serving such traditional English fare as roast beef and two veg... The two Frenchwomen who had bought an Afratan retreat for their holidays found their ownership of its tiny patch of garden hotly disputed by the owner of an adjacent house... A relative in Germany sent Kyriacos an electronic sphygmomanometer that, until the novelty wore off, was the talk of kafeneon society. Most of the village's old boys tried the apparently miraculous device and then took an almost morbid delight in public discussion of their blood pressure readings... We declined the offer of some more land when the price was revealed to be 20 times what it was worth. The seller allowed a decent interval to pass and then contritely said that his wife had chastised him for asking so much – we could have it if we would pay only 10 times what it was worth... Stratis, Kyriacos's neighbour, retired off both his donkey and his *patateri*. Today, neither is to be seen, although, as I write, the donkey's traditional wooden saddle lies abandoned by the roadside. Perhaps I should go and pick it up before a passing souvenir-hunter spots it...

You are invited

...to renew your acquaintance with Pug and Mavros, the "whoopee cushions" from STILL LIFE IN CRETE. The two philosopher-pugs have their own weekly cartoon strip at www.inkmonitor.com, where you can read their thoughts – which range across life's menu from Antipasto to Zabaglione – and see for yourself that there is indeed intelligent life on the hearth!

R.S.V.P www.inkmonitor.com

3+1
Simple Greek Recipes

FAVA   *yellow split-pea purée or soup* (to serve 4-6)

If Napoleon's army marched on its stomach, the Greeks went to war on yellow split peas. Yiannis Dagounakis says that he has two abiding memories of his wartime experiences in Albania: the cold, which nearly cost him his life, and *fava* – which kept him going. This nourishing meal-in-a-pot – a staple of the original Cretan diet – is undoubtedly one of the simplest and most sustaining dishes in the modern Greek cook's armoury!

Ingredients
500 gm yellow split peas
1 large onion, finely sliced
250 ml olive oil
salt and pepper

Method
Pick over and wash the split peas. Put them in a large saucepan and cover them with water. Bring to the boil and skim off any scum that forms. When the water is clear, add the finely-sliced onion and olive oil and gently simmer. Cook for about an hour, stirring occasionally (but more frequently towards the end to stop the purée sticking to the saucepan) and adding water if necessary. The *fava* is ready when the peas have completely lost their shape and the purée has the consistency of soft porridge. Add salt and

pepper to taste and stir very thoroughly to make as smooth as possible.

To Serve:
100-200 ml olive oil (to taste)
1 medium onion, finely chopped (red onion is preferred – or experiment with scallions)
juice of 1-2 lemons
chopped parsley, rocket or capers (optional)

Pour the purée into a shallow serving bowl and allow to cool a little. Beat together the lemon juice and olive oil and pour half of it over the *fava*. Sprinkle on some of the chopped onion (and herbs if using). Serve it warm like a soup – or cold like a paté – with plenty of crusty bread and the remaining oil, lemon juice and onions on the side. *A generous quantity of top-quality olive oil (preferably Cretan) is essential to the success of this dish.*

ΓΑΣΣΟLΑΔΑ *bean soup or stew* (to serve 6)

Fassolada – the Greek equivalent of Jewish chicken soup and barley – is every Cretan mother's favourite winter warmer. The Greeks claim that they invented thick soup and the classic *fassolada* is the epitome of the genre. It's a substantial meal on its own, and a recorded favourite of Ancient Athenians (past and present!).

Ingredients
250 gm haricot beans
250 ml olive oil
1-2 large onions, finely sliced
4 medium carrots, finely chopped
2 medium sticks of celery, finely chopped, plus a handful of leaves
1 leek (optional)
2-3 cloves of garlic, sliced

3 medium tomatoes, peeled and roughly chopped
small bunch of parsley
1 teaspoon tomato paste
½ teaspoon dried thyme or oregano
salt and pepper
red wine vinegar (optional)

Method
Soak the beans in plenty of cold water *for at least six hours*. Then put them in a large pan, cover with water and bring to the boil. Boil for a few minutes, then drain the beans and keep them on one side. Rinse the pan and put it back on the heat with about 2/3 of the olive oil, the onions, celery sticks, carrots, garlic (and leek if using). Sauté the vegetables for a few minutes, until they soften. Add the beans, half the parsley, roughly chopped, the thyme or oregano and one litre of water. When the saucepan comes to the boil, lower the heat to a gentle simmer and cook for an hour. Add the tomatoes and tomato paste and continue cooking until the beans are soft but not breaking up. Add salt and pepper to taste, the remaining olive oil and parsley – and a dash of red wine vinegar.

CRETAN PILAFI (to serve 6-8)

Pilafi is the traditional dish for special occasions, such as weddings and baptisms. In the past, these were the events which justified the slaughtering of an animal – and the meat was boiled because the animal might not have been particularly young! *Pilafi* is made from lamb or chicken, and sometimes from a mixture of both. It is an easy dish to make in large quantities – if you have a large enough pan; Cretan cooks generally use one the size of a dustbin! They also add a lot more butter than is recommended in this recipe…

Ingredients
1 chicken (a boiling fowl is tastiest)
1 large onion
small bunch of parsley
a few celery leaves
1 bay leaf
salt and pepper
risotto-type rice (1 teacup-full per person)
1 tablespoon of butter per person
lemon juice to taste

Method
Place the chicken in a large pan and cover with cold water. Bring to the boil and skim the water until clear. Add the onion, roughly cut up, and the parsley, celery leaves and bay leaf tied together with some thread, plus salt and pepper to taste. Simmer until tender (1-2 hours according to the age of the bird). Lift out the chicken, cut into serving pieces, cover and keep warm. Strain and measure the broth into a clean pan – 3 cups of broth for every cup of rice. Bring to the boil and throw in the rice. Boil over a medium heat until done, stirring occasionally and adding more broth or water if the rice seems to be getting too dry. It should have the consistency of a risotto rather than being dry and separately grained. Adjust seasoning, if necessary, then heat the butter until the foam subsides and pour it over the rice. Add lemon juice to taste and serve the chicken pieces on top of the rice.

SƐMOLIИA HALVA *sweet and simple*

Crete is a dessert-ed island when it comes to after-dinner "puddings". Bakers' shops and *zakaroplasteia* sell the world's gooiest confections but sweet things only rarely find their way on to a *taverna* or *estiatorio* menu. There is, however, one occasional exception, *halva*, which, when it's available, is generally served *gratis* along with a small glass of *tschikoudia* – and your bill.

Ingredients
75 gm butter (or margarine)
75 gm pine nuts (substitute flaked almonds, if necessary)
125 gm semolina
For the syrup:
150 gm white sugar
450 ml water
150 ml milk
1 cinnamon stick
+ a little ground cinnamon for sprinkling

Method
Boil the ingredients for the syrup in a heavy pan for 5 minutes and then set aside. In a large saucepan or frying pan, melt the butter and lightly brown the pine nuts. Add the semolina and fry the mixture over a medium heat, stirring all the time, until it becomes a deep golden colour (after about 10 minutes). Remove the pan from the heat, take the cinnamon stick out of the syrup and *carefully* pour the syrup over the hot semolina. Return the pan to a gentle heat and stir until all the liquid has been absorbed but the mixture still looks moist. Take the pan off the heat, cover it with a clean tea towel and a lid and leave to stand for about 10 minutes. If it is to be eaten warm, fluff it up with a fork and serve immediately, sprinkled with a little ground cinnamon. If it is to be eaten cold, spread it lightly into a greased dish or tin so that it is 2 or 3 cm deep. Sprinkle it lightly with cinnamon and, when cold, cut it into squares. It is delicious served with creamy Greek yoghurt.

Printed in the United Kingdom
by Lightning Source UK Ltd.
9625800001B